Benjamin Franklin DeCosta

The Northmen in Maine

A critical Examination of Views expressed in Connection with the Subject

Benjamin Franklin DeCosta

The Northmen in Maine

A critical Examination of Views expressed in Connection with the Subject

ISBN/EAN: 9783743331358

Manufactured in Europe, USA, Canada, Australia, Japa

Cover: Foto ©ninafisch / pixelio.de

Manufactured and distributed by brebook publishing software (www.brebook.com)

Benjamin Franklin DeCosta

The Northmen in Maine

THE

Northmen in Maine;

A

CRITICAL EXAMINATION

OF

VIEWS EXPRESSED IN CONNECTION WITH THE
SUBJECT, BY DR. J. H. KOHL,

IN

VOLUME I OF THE NEW SERIES OF THE MAINE
HISTORICAL SOCIETY.

TO WHICH ARE ADDED

CRITICISMS ON OTHER PORTIONS OF THE WORK,

AND A CHAPTER ON THE

Discovery of Massachusetts Bay.

BY THE

REV. B. F. DECOSTA,
AUTHOR OF THE PRE-COLUMBIAN DISCOVERY OF AMERICA
BY THE NORTHMEN, ETC., ETC.

ALBANY:
JOEL MUNSELL.
1870.

PREFATORY NOTE.

The following papers were prepared with reference to their publication in one of the leading periodicals; but a further consideration of the subject led to the opinion that a separate presentation would more effectually secure the object which the author had in view. The papers are, nevertheless, sent forth nearly in their original form.

Stuyvesant Park.

New York, September, 1869.

NORTHMEN IN MAINE.

The new volume of the Maine Historical Society, containing as it does no less than twenty-six ancient maps relating to the coast of America, forms a valuable companion to the student of history located at a distance from the large libraries. And yet the volume is open to serious criticism. One naturally feels that this is entering upon an unwelcome task, especially as the author is a foreigner and a distinguished scholar. For the talents and attainments of Dr. Kohl we entertain high admiration, and yet errors coming from such a source are doubly injurious, and, more than all others, demand refutation. Indeed, it is quite evident from the distinguished author's laborious efforts to set forth the truth of history that he will not object to the essays of others, even when the result may displace his own conclusions.

With these remarks, offered to obviate any possible misunderstanding of the writer's motives, let us proceed to examine the work of the latter, especially in its relation to the Northmen and the State of Maine.

The only expedition of the Northmen which Dr. Kohl tries to connect with Maine is that of the distinguished Icelander, Thorfinn Karlsefne. Let us, therefore, hear what he says, keeping in mind the fact that Dr. Kohl and the writer agree perfectly in regard to the locality of the places referred to in the sagas, accepting Markland as Nova Scotia, Kialarness as Cape Cod, and so on to the end. With this preliminary remark, let us hear what Dr. Kohl says. On page 71 of his work, he writes as follows of the voyage of Karlsefne, which was begun in 1007, instead of 1008:

"From Markland (Nova Scotia), they did not go out to the open sea, through the broad part of the Gulf of Maine, as had been done on the former expeditions; but they coasted along a great way *to the south-west, having the land always on their starboard*' until they at length came to Kialarness (Cape Cod)." This is supplemented by the remark:

"Thorfinn and Gudrida, in following this track, probably wished to find the place where Thorwald had been buried, and his crosses erected, which they of course knew were to be found on the coast toward the north of Cape Cod."

Consequently, he arrives at the conclusion that: "We have here the first coasting voyage of European navigators along the shores of Maine."

Now it must be observed, first, that this alleged voyage involved a large departure from the direct course. The expeditionists were sailing to Vinland, Massachusetts and

Rhode Island, being in small vessels, with live stock on board, and everything necessary to found a colony. This being so, they would not deviate from their course without good reason. Dr. Kohl felt this, and hence suggests a motive for the alleged departure. He, as already quoted, says that in "following this track, Thorfinn wished to find the place where Thorwald had been buried." This person was killed four years previous, but why would they desire to find the spot? Thorfinn had just been married, and it is not very likely that his wife would desire to take him now on a pilgrimage to her brother-in-law's grave. Her first husband had endeavored to bring home Thorwald's body to Greenland, yet this expedition did not propose anything of the kind.

It was also definitely settled that they should proceed to the spot where Leif had already built houses in Vinland. There was, therefore, no reason or propriety in sailing first to visit the grave of Thorwald. Yet this is the only motive suggested. It is hardly necessary to say that it was utterly insufficient.

But now, for the sake of the argument, supposing Thorfinn had been influenced by this motive, is it likely that he would have taken the course alleged? Dr. Kohl says, that "they of course knew that the crosses marking Thorwald's grave, were to be found on the coast towards the north of Cape Cod." But here he is at variance, not only with the sagas, but with *himself*. According to his own statement, the fight in which Thorwald was killed, took place "near the harbor of Boston," and it is said in the saga that his body was carried back *southward* to a cape and buried; to this Dr. Kohl necessarily assents. This cape, "Crossness," was probably Gurnet Point, Plymouth, as generally conceded. At all events the burial place was *south* of Boston and *west* of Cape Cod, and yet Dr. Kohl tells us that they "of course, knew that the crosses were on the coast, towards the north of Cape Cod," and pictures them sailing along the Maine shore, with their eyes upon the coast in search of the crosses of Thorwald. This is what no sensible man like Thorfinn Karlsefne would be guilty of, especially when we remember Dr. Kohl's own words, where he says, "they no doubt had some of Thorwald's former companions on board." These people well understood that in order to reach the grave of Thorwald they must sail direct for Kialarness, the end of Cape Cod, and then push on to the west. Cape Cod was their *first land-fall* in seeking Crossness (Gurnet Point), which being the case, we have no reason to suppose that they sailed along the coast of Maine searching for crosses that they *knew were not there.*

There is, therefore, nothing in the *motive urged,* or the *course alleged to have been fol-*

lowed, which leads to the belief that, "we have here the first coasting voyage of European navigators along the coast of Maine."

But is there anything in the *language of the narrative* which implies that on this occasion they sailed out of the ordinary course?

Dr. Kohl assumes this to be so, yet we must examine the authority. We quote his language again: " They coasted along a great way '*to the south-west, having the land always on their starboard*,' until they came to Kialarness." As authority for this, we have, in a note, a Danish translation of the original Icelandic, yet neither this Danish translation, nor the original, bears out the English of Dr. Kohl. (*Antiq. Amer.*, p. 139).

But we must note farther, that he says Thorfinn sailed south-west a long way "*until* they at length came to Kialarness." Much is made to depend upon the word "until," it being required in order to make perfectly sure that they coasted along the shores of Maine, and thus gave us this "first voyage." But "until," in the Icelandic is *ok*. Rafn in his Danish, gives *og*, and in the Latin *et*, simply *and*. If the Icelandic *ok* meant "until," we should require in the Danish *indtif*, and in the Latin *utque*. But the original *ok* is plain, and the word used, "until," is unwarrantable.

It is said, it will be observed, that they sailed from Markland (Nova Scotia), to the south-west, having the land "*always* on the starboard." And this "always" is needed in order to make the expedition *appear* to be running down the Maine coast. But the Icelandic simply says that "the land was on the right" (*La landit a Stjorn*), which is rendered by Rafn, *Terra ab dextro navis latere jacuit*. The Danish was before Dr. Kohl's eyes on his own page, and to exactly the same effect. Hence, where does he get the "always"? It is simply imagined.

Yet even this is not all, for in Dr. Kohl's account the several parts of the sentence are put out of their right relation. A fair translation would read thus:

"They sailed long southward by the land, and came to a cape; the land lay on the right." This is the order and punctuation of the original; from which it appears that they sailed an indefinite distance *and* came to a cape; which, being done, they found that the land *then* lay upon their right. This, it will be perceived, is a very different thing from saying, that they sailed along by the land to the cape (Cape Cod), with the land *always* upon their right. In the latter case they *must* have followed the shores, and therefore coasted along the shores of Maine, while in the former it is not necessary.

But, perhaps, it may be thought that the language after all fairly bears the construction placed upon it, when properly translated. We read: "They sailed long south by the land, and came to a cape; the land lay on the right." One might say that the land which "lay on the right," was a part of the coast that they sailed by, yet the grammatical construction does not require it, while the elliptical construction of Icelandic narrative will not permit it. Before the words, "and came to a cape," there should be a full stop. This would give the sense more clearly, as *now*, things that we shall yet see to be perfectly distinct, are loosely run together.

But what is still worse for this interpretation, is the fact that the interpretation proposed is *totally* unsuited to a description of a voyage from Nova Scotia down the coast of Maine; for, after rounding Cape Sable, they would be obliged to sail northward, and cross the bay of Fundy, where they would lose the land for a long distance, or else cut clear of the land altogether, and sail west by north about two hundred miles to the region of the Kennebec. The language, therefore, is totally unsuited to meet the wants of this alleged coasting voyage of Europeans on the coast of Maine, as the map proves.

It will be perceived that in all that has gone before I have met Dr. Kohl on his own ground, and allowed that when Thorfinn sailed south to Kialarness (Cape Cod), he started "from Markland" (Nova Scotia). But there is still another error that lies at the bottom of all the rest. Dr. Kohl says, in his haste, that they sailed "from Markland," whereas they did *not* sail from "Markland."

Let us hear what the saga says. After mentioning the fact that Thorfinn Karlsefne's expedition first touched Helluland (Labrador), it goes on to say : " Then they sailed a day and a night in a southerly course, and came to a land covered with woods, in which there were many wild beasts. Beyond this land to the south-east lay an island on which they slew a bear. They called the island

Bear Island, and the land Markland. *Thence they sailed south long by the land, and came to a cape; the land lay on the right side,*" etc. (*Antiq. Amer.*, p. 138).

It therefore appears that the *last* place touched at was not Markland, but the island, and that from *thence* they sailed southward. And the importance of this correction will be evident, when we see that the right interpretation of the whole passage depends upon it. In fact, it gives a new point of departure. Therefore, where was this island? The location depends upon the part of Nova Scotia upon which they landed. It is said that it lay south-west of Markland, and hence it must have been one of the many islands, that lie along the coast. And supposing, as we reasonably may, that they touched first on or near the northern half of Nova Scotia, we *then* have a long coast for them to sail past, after they left the outlying island. It would not indeed give them the land "always" on the right "until" they came to the cape (Cape Cod), as Dr. Kohl says, yet we have already shown that nothing like the equivalent of these words are to be found in the original. As we have also observed, the saga is elliptical in its style, and that the punctuation of the *printed* Icelandic *text* required a period before the words, "and came to a cape." The simple truth is, that they sailed, not "from Markland," as Dr. Kohl so hastily concludes, but from the isle called "Bear Island," having the coast of Markland (Nova Scotia), on their right for a long way; after which they left it, and next struck the coast of Cape Cod, leaving Maine and New Hampshire undiscovered far on the right. It is therefore perfectly clear that this, the first alleged coasting voyage by Europeans on the Maine coast never took place. Yet lest any one should be disposed to raise a quibble, I will produce another testimony, by means of which alone, the question might have been settled at the start; yet it was due to the subject to view it from every point of view, and hence I have delayed the testimony referred to until now.

The distinguished German, in his discussion of Karlsefne's voyage, has based his theory upon what is called "The Narrative of Thorfinn Karlsefne," written in Iceland, and preserved in the *Arnœ-Magnean Collection*. But fortunately we have another version, contained in the Saga of Eric the Red, which makes still clearer what the first narrative may, to some, seem to leave in doubt. This is called, "The Account of Thorfinn." It was written in Greenland, and is of equal value with the other.

In order to set the question in its final aspect before the reader, we give the passage from "The Account of Thorfinn," which is parallel with that already examined. After stating the departure from Helluland (Nova Scotia), the language is as follows:

"They came to a land in which there were great woods and many animals. Southeast, opposite the land, lay an island. Here they found a bear, and called the island Bear Island. This land where there were woods, they called Markland. After a voyage of a day and a night[1] *they discovered* (or saw), *land*, and they sailed near the land, and saw that it was a cape. They kept close to the shore with the wind on the right (starboard) side, and left (or *had*) the land upon the right side of the ship."

Now by a careful comparison it will be seen that this version harmonizes completely with the first, and at the same time shows, with greater distinctness, that they left the land at Nova Scotia, after sailing by it some time, and saw the land again *first* at Cape Cod. Thus this alleged voyage disappears.

---

[1] The long day is here meant.

We finally have to notice what Dr. Kohl has to say about Thorhall, who was in the expedition of Karlsefne, and who left the latter at the Rhode Island settlement to go around Cape Cod. Dr. Kohl falls into error at the outset, saying that "Thorfinn had *sent* to the north from Straumfiord (Buzzard's Bay), his man, Thorhall the Hunter." The truth is, however, that we have no intimation of Thorhall being "sent." On the contrary, this episode appears to have been against the wishes of Thorfinn.

In summing up the result of Thorhall's voyage, Dr. Kohl is equally unfortunate, and says, that he made his exploring expedition "to the northern parts of Vinland (coast of Maine)." But the narrative simply says (in two versions), that Thorhall "sailed north to go around Wonder Strand and Kialarness [Cape Cod], but when he wished to sail westward [towards Plymouth, Mass.], they were met by a storm and driven back."

Thus he did not even weather Race Point, Provincetown, and yet we are told that he made an expedition to the " coast of Maine," (p. 80).

Afterwards, when Thorhall did not return, having been forced to run for the coast of Ireland, Thorfinn went in search of him. This voyage northward, from Rhode Island, Dr. Kohl also, unluckily, turns into an expedition to Maine, though he does not say how far they went, only remarking that it "might have been somewhere in the inner parts of the gulf of Maine."

Nevertheless we very well know that Thorfinn did not go near Maine, nor even far north of Boston. The saga says that he "sailed northward [from Rhode Island], past Kialarness, and then westward [to Plymouth shore], and the land was upon their larboard (left) side." They finally reached a river, where they anchored, and then went northward again. Dr. Kohl says we do not know how far, but that the point reached might have been "somewhere in the *inner parts* of the Gulf of Maine" (p. 76). Nevertheless his *own quotation* from the saga intimates, on the contrary, that they know how far north they went, saying, "all these tracts to the north were continuous with those in the south, and that it was all one and the same country."

Now this extract shows that there was something in the physical character of the country which enabled the Northmen to perceive its identity with the country of Maine. Yet, supposing with Dr. Kohl they had reached the coast of Maine, which lies on the "inner part" of the "gulf," what is there to be seen by which they could infer that it was "all one and the same country" with that "at Hop"? Evidently, nothing; and, therefore, the inference of Karlsefne, if made on the Maine coast, would have had no force. And yet there was something in the physical character of the country between that and the place where they were, which, like a thread running through a piece of French print, being now the eye of a beast, and now the petal of a rose, was easily recognized. What therefore *was* this feature? This was nothing less than a *mountain range*, which is not hinted at in Dr. Kohl's glaringly false translation above given. A true translation would run: "They considered the *mountain range* that was at Hop, and that which they now found as all one." The Icelandic word translated "*tracts*," by Dr. Kohl is *Fjöll*, the equivalent of which in Danish is *Fjeldstrækning*, or mountain range, inadequately expressed in the Latin *montes*. Therefore, in order to learn how far they went, we have only to ascertain how far the range beginning at Mount Hope bay (Hop), extends northward. Any good county map settles this question, and reveals the fact that the range ends in the Milton Blue hills, seen from the vicinity of Boston Harbor, and mentioned in Blunt's *Coast Pilot*. *Therefore the northward limit of this voyage must be fixed in the latitude of Boston*. Antiq. Amer., p. xxxv.

That Thorfinn and his men were thoroughly qualified to give an opinion, appears from the fact that the summer before, they had "decided to explore all the mountains in Hop; *which done*," the saga continues, " they went and passed the third winter in Straumfiord" (Buzzard's bay). They also state in connection with the fact that the range seen was "all one" with that at Hop, that it also " appeared to be of equal length from Straumfiord to both places," a judgment also seen to be tolerably correct, from Rafn's map, which makes the three points mentioned nearly the points of a triangle. The narrative it therefore perfectly consistent and clear. The river that they entered was probably near Scituate harbor, and when they drew northward to the vicinity of

Boston, Blue Hill range plainly appeared, and was easily recognized as a part of the mountain range that they had already explored by land from the south.

Thus, by a legitimate rendering of the language of the sagas, the alleged voyages of the Northmen upon and to the coast of Maine in the eleventh century totally disappear. If they made any voyages at a later period, which is not impossible, they left no record of the fact, and the "first Europeans" who coasted those shores, must be looked for elsewhere than among the Northmen.

In conclusion we have to notice several points not immediately connected with Maine, which nevertheless serve to show how hastily the whole subject was disposed of.

Dr. Kohl says (p. 77), "It is not quite clear, but it appears to me probable,[1] that a

---

[1] Elsewhere (p. 478), he says, "Their colonies in America, first in Vinland and Markland, then in Greenland, declined."

party of his [Karlsefne's] men remained behind and continued the settlement." For this statement there is no authority whatever. When the second summer of his sojourn in Vinland came, Karlsefne decided to abandon the undertaking. The following year the whole party left. (*Antiquitates Americanæ*, p. 156). The statements all agree to this effect, and we have information in regard to the departure of each of the three ships. Moreover, when Freydis fitted out her expedition, which took place on the year of Karlsefne's return, she stipulated with Leif that she should have the use of the empty houses in Vinland which he had built. On the arrival of Freydis she took possession, and the whole account gives additional proof that Karlsefne left none of his party behind.

Again, Dr. Kohl says (p. 83), "This priest [Bishop Eric], is said to have sailed to Vinland for missionary purposes." But by *whom* is he "said" to have sailed for this purpose? All that we have about this voyage is the simple statement, that, in the year 1121, Bishop Eric went to "search" for or "seek out," Vinland (*Antiquitates Americanæ*, p. 261). From this statement it has been unfortunately argued that a settlement existed in New England at the time, and that Eric went to superintend ecclesiastical affairs. With this fancy as a foundation, Prof. Rafn, in his early enthusiasm, connected the Newport Mill with the ancient colonists, and indulged in the belief that the structure in question was a baptistery. (See Supplement to *Antiquitates Americanæ*). This was only a fancy, as the language of the statement implies that the knowledge of Vinland was lost.

Again it said (page 78), that " Freydisa and her companions got into trouble and disagreement, probably about the profits of the undertaking. They came to arms, and the two brothers, Helge and Finnboge, were slain in a fight." But here again Dr. Kohl shows only a portion of the truth. There is not the slightest grounds for the supposition that they quarreled about the "profits." The ill feeling began by Freydis' violation of the compact that the ships should carry an equal number of men. Again, on reaching Vinland there was a quarrel about the possession of the houses, Freydis claiming their exclusive use. Then, when winter came, they quarreled in the midst of their games, which were abandoned. Eventually she complained to her husband that Finnboge and Helge had struck and abused her. Accordingly Thorwald, her husband, went with his men early one morning to the huts of the two brothers, seized them and their company in their beds, bound them and led them out and murdered them. The women of Finnboge's party were slain by Freydis herself, as the humanity of her followers would not permit them to go farther in this horrible butchery. Freydis returned and reported the brothers and their company lost, and thus possessed herself of property that was not rightfully hers (see *Pre-Columbian Discovery*, pp. 77–80, and *Antiquitates Americanæ*, pp. 65–72).

After failing thus on points where there is such abundant testimony, it is easy to understand how he would have obtained a wrong impression on points that are somewhat critical.

THE CHART OF THE ZENO BROTHERS.

While there is much in the work of Dr. Kohl that justifies criticism, it is nevertheless gratifying to find him conceding the authenticity of the chart drawn up by Nicolo and Antonio Zeno, prior to the year 1400. Yet something must be said in this connection, though the discussion does not tend directly upon the history of Maine.

First we have to regret that in transcribing this chart, Dr. Kohl has failed to give the best representation possible. No less than one-half of the Greenland names have been dropped altogether, though these are names that inevitably come under discussion when the question of authenticity arrives at the crucial point. Concerning those actually left, he says nothing, and refers to the distinguished Polish geographer, Lelewel, for all the needed information. He does this, after going over the other portions of the chart, explaining the names, and demonstrating their alleged antiquity. He tells us that the Greenland names are of less interest for his purpose, but what was the purpose of the discussion? Manifestly it was either to illustrate the history of Maine, or to prove the authenticity of the chart. If the former, then the Greenland names were equally pertinent with the others; while if it was the latter, the discussion of the Greenland names were far more so. This, it is believed, can be fully demonstrated, yet Dr. Kohl takes leave of the subject at this point and refers to Lelewel. Turning, therefore, to the eminent Polish writer, what do we find? Nothing less than this, that he has really obscured the subject, with which he does not grapple, not having made it a study.

The names given by the Zeni in connection with other portions of the map are names that probably could not have been obtained in 1558 (when the map was printed), by a person engaged in a fabrication; but those names connected with the Greenland coast are names that were less likely to have been obtained. Hence the peculiar interest.

Again, at the late period referred to, it was impossible to rightly apply the names in question. We find that Greenland was first settled by Icelandic colonists in the year 985, and that the settlements continued for over three hundred years, when they died out, and the knowledge of Greenland was practically lost. The location of the settlements even became a matter of doubt. Hence we find Torfæus in his work on Old Greenland, placing nearly all the towns and villages on the east coast. In so doing he acted upon what he and all his colaborers mistook for the meaning of *Bardsen's Chroni-*

cle, which gives the best account of the ancient colonies now extant. Torfæus published his work in 1715, and was followed by map-makers down to a comparatively recent period. Indeed, it was no later than the year 1828 that the Danish government sent out an expedition to Greenland under Captain Graah,[1] to settle the question concerning the former existence of a colony on the east coast. His researches had the effect of banishing the last ray of hope that might have been entertained. Wormskiold was the latest Scandinavian scholar who seriously advocated the view that the East Bygd lay on the east coast, where he thought a remnant of the colony might still exist, shut in by the ice. But when the Society of Northern Antiquarians, profiting by explorations in Greenland, set out upon their

---

[1] For convenience sake, the author would refer to the discussion of the subject in his work on *Pre-Columbian Discovery*.

great work, the modern maps were revised and *both* the districts were placed on the west side, according to Bardsen, a *relative* distinction of east and west only being maintained, as will be seen by a glance at their maps published in 1837. And this constituted nothing less than a most *striking confession of the truth of the Zeni chart*, which locates the settlements on the west side. Theodore Thorlacius[1] (1668), innocently mutilated the Greenland section, which was drawn with a degree of correctness that would alone go far to vindicate the antiquity of the work, while Mercator and Ortelius in constructing their maps took an equal

---

[1] See Torfæus's *Gronlandia Antiqua*, Havniæ, 1715, where also may be seen the map of Stephanius (1570), and that of Bishop Gudbrand Torlacius (1606). Those men, like the rest, misunderstood the chronicle of Ivar Bardsen, owing to the almost complete extinction of geographical knowledge relating to Greenland. The Zeni, however, were familiar with those regions, as their chart proves.

amount of liberty with other portions. Yet in the end these mutilations were wholly rejected.

It will thus be seen that the Zeni knew where the colonies lay, and, notwithstanding a partial confusion of names, which the ravages of time increased on the original map, the fact is clearly demonstrable.

It would have been a strong point gained, if this map had simply shown that the Icelandic colonies of Greenland were *not on the east side*. But, in addition to this, it proves that they were on the *west*.[1] This is clearly seen from the fact that of all the names put on the east side *we cannot recognize one that*

---

[1] Still the light on this point travels slowly. The American Antiquarian Society, in 1860, published the following: "Intercourse with that part of Greenland which was colonized by the Danes, has been prevented by ice since the beginning of the fifteenth century," (vol. IV, p. 269, N. 2). The part alluded to is the east coast. The Danes, of course, had nothing to do with colonizing any part of Greenland.

anciently belonged to the west side. Lelewel, in his invaluable work, *Geographie du Moyen age* (*tom.* III, p. 98), indeed confounds two names that appear on the east coast with names that belong to the west. Yet whoever consults that part of his examination of the Zeni map will perceive that he did not appreciate the interest that really clusters around the Greenland names, and failed to give them the attention that they deserved. His remarks on the Greenland names are barren of interest. He seeks chiefly to give the equivalent of Zeno's names in modern terms, and in so doing falls into a most palpable error. Two names on the east are *fl.* (*fluvium*) *Lande*, and *pr.* (*promontory*) *Hien*, one of which he makes identical with Einersfiord, and the other with Heriulfsness, while *both* of those places were located on the west coast. Why, then, did he make this interpretation? Certainly there was nothing in the names themselves to authorize it. It was, therefore, simply a mistake, into which he fell, when giving, in a separate column, certain modern names whose places generally correspond with those of the chart.[1]

It is not proposed in this connection to examine the names placed by the Zeni on the west coast. In order to explain all of them it would be necessary to have access to the manuscripts containing the various versions of Bardsen's relation; and even then the effort would not be wholly crowned with success, since in many cases the names have been so corrupted. All that is now required is to show that the Zeni located the colonies on the west coast. This, after the correction

---

[1] There is another name put by the Zeni on the east coast, *pr. Munder*, which Lelewel defines as Lodmund, the name of a fiord on the west coast: Yet the same name was often given to several things as well as places. But it must be remembered there was only *one* Ericsfiord and one Heriulfsness. As Lelewell remarks, Brattahlid and Garda, very prominent places, do not appear on the map; yet other names just as useful for our purpose *do* appear.

of Lelewel's mistake, is easily done, as will appear from a mere glance. We see, among other things, that they understood what has required so much modern study to elucidate, namely: that in sailing to Greenland, the Icelander passed *two* Huarfs,[1] or turning points, one being at Cape Farewell and the other some distance up the east coast; while the names of places, as given by Bardsen, are recognized, *Eleste,* for instance, among others, a name that has needlessly been deemed obscure, but which is nevertheless the remnant of "Henlestate."[2]

Everything, therefore, points indisputably to the antiquity of the Zeni Chart; for we must remember again, that in 1558, when the chart was published, the ancient geography

---

[1] By referring to Zurla's copy of the map, this will be more apparent, as Lelewel in copying the two names gets them misspelled. Zurla was, manifestly, the more careful in handling these two names.

[2] See *Sailing Directions of Henry Hudson,* p. 76.

of Greenland had reached the period of deepest obscuration, a period that cast its shadow forward into the next century, when, in 1668, Theodore Thorlacius drew up the worst chart of Greenland ever offered to the public. At no time between 1500 and 1675, does it appear to have been *suspected* by Icelandic geographers that settlements ever existed on Greenland's western coast. Hence, on the charts we find them laying down localities on the east coast that actually belonged to the region of Lancaster sound! Fortunately, ere this period of darkness set in, and while voyages were often made from the northern parts of Europe to Greenland, the Zeni brothers improved the opportunities afforded by their journeys to put upon parchment those leading facts which lend to their testimony the seal of truth,[1] and which en-

---

[1] It will of course be understood that the writer does not by any means accept everything stated in the *narratives* of the Zeni, which both illustrate and obscure

title them to rank among the Pre-Columbian Explorers of America.

Of the value of this map, in its connection with Maine, little needs to be said. In his copy, Dr. Kohl has colored Drogeo, which in one place (p. 105), he suggests as covering New England, while in another (p. 478), he says, "Maine is put down under the name of Drogeo." A note (p. 106), also says that in Lelewel's copy, Drogeo occupies exactly the locality of the territory of Maine, which seems to imply that the masses of land were differently grouped on the map of the Polish geographer. This is not the case. In *all* the copies that have come under the author's notice, Drogeo is represented on 58° and 59° north. The lines of latitude, how-

---

their chart. Like all similar relations, they will justify a careful sifting. The contrast between the chart and the narratives is most notable. The former contains but a single false feature in its Greenland section, namely: the monastery of St. Thomas, placed on the coast to the north of Iceland.

ever, are of no authority. Remembering this, still Drogeo is always put in the above latitude, which is ten degrees north of the extreme limit of the territory of Maine.[1] The map, therefore, has no interest in connection with Maine, as might be said of the two following Icelandic maps of the volume. And it may well be observed in this connection, that it would be difficult to say when the territory of Maine first clearly emerges in the old cartology. It has already been suggested by one critic,[2] that Cosa's map of 1500 indicates the coast of Asia instead of Maine, as supposed by Dr. Kohl. Thorne, in his letter to Henry VIII, urges the same view with regard to that region, which he claimed as the India possessions of the British crown. (See Hak-

---

[1] Henry Stevens, G. M. B., F. S. A., etc., in "*Historical and Geographical Notes*, 1453–1869," p. 19, n.

[2] Perhaps, it will be said, that the unrepresented part was in the locality of Maine, yet the unknown is something that we cannot speculate about.

luyt, vol. I, p. 213, ed. 1598). If Dr. Kohl is right in his supposed discovery of Cape Cod on Cosa's map, he is also right with reference to Maine; yet the island which he identifies with Nantucket is on the wrong side of the cape, which in the eleventh century doubtless had a small outlying island toward the east, as indicated by Saga of Karlsefne, and proved by more recent history, in connection with geological surveys.[1] Yet it is not worth while to appear fanciful, as we require truth on the chart as well as on the written page. The map of the Zeni, however, is authenticated, which would seem enough, without applying it to Maine.

---

[1] See *Pre-Columbian Discovery*, p. 26, n. The shores and banks of Georges are probably dead islands that once lifted themselves above the sea.

THE VOYAGE OF JOHN RUT.

In the year 1527, an English expedition, composed of two ships, the Sampson and the Mary of Guilford, was sent into American waters. In the course of the voyage, it is asserted by Dr. Kohl, John Rut, the master of the Mary of Guilford, visited the shores of Maine; and he tells us that in the account of Hakluyt (vol. III, p. 129, ed. 1600), we have "information of the first instance in which Englishmen are certainly known to have *put their feet on these shores.*"

But upon what is this claim based? Quoting from Hakluyt, he says that the Mary of Guilford "returned by the coasts of New Foundland, Cape Breton and Norumbega," often "entering the ports of those regions, landing men, and examining into the condition of the country" (*Dr. Kohl*, p. 283).

Now the oldest reference to Norumbega is found in the work of Peter Martyr (*Dec.* VII, c. 11), which appeared about 1511. It is next mentioned in a "Discourse of a great French sea-captain of Dieppe, on the navigations made to the West Indies, called New France, from the 40° to the 47° N.," given in Ramusio (vol. III, p. 423). This discourse has been attributed to Pierre Crignon, the poet, and seems to belong to the year 1539, from the fact that the writer says that fifteen years had then elapsed since Verazzano made his voyage. He tells us that the country from Cape Breton to Florida is called by the inhabitants Norumbega.

But, though the application of the name was thus extensive, it never figured largely upon the maps. The name appears to have come in *northward* from the St. Lawrence. Hence, in 1556, the pilots told Thevet that

Norumbega was the "proper country of Canada" (*Cosmographie Universelle*, 1004). And we must not fail to notice the fact that the very map that Crignon's account was intended to illustrate (*Gastaldi's*, 1550), restricts the country of Norumbega to Nova Scotia. Nevertheless it is conceded that the maps do not tell the whole story of Norumbega, which was taken to include the country from Cape Breton to Florida. By degrees, the application of the term was narrowed, until it came to signify a fabulous city on Penobscot river, in Maine. Yet what was the meaning of the term when Hakluyt wrote? This is easily ascertained. Dr. Kohl himself admits the fatal truth, that in Hakluyt's day all New England was included in Norumbega. But more than this. Turning to the account of Sir Humphrey Gilbert's expedition, we find one of the members speaking of it as put on foot for "the discovery of Norumbega." And yet the plan of the voyage aimed at a thorough exploration of the territory from Newfoundland to Florida. This shows that in 1583, Norumbega still had a very wide application, while it is equally certain that Nova Scotia was *always* included at the time Hakluyt wrote. (See *Hakluyt*, vol. III, p. 163; also title page of same volume). It will therefore, be seen, when Dr. Kohl quotes Hakluyt as saying Rut returned to England "by the coasts" of Norumbega, that he *proves nothing*, for *we do not know what part of Norumbega he landed upon*. Taking the term applied to New England in general, as Dr. Kohl admits it was used, there is still no certainty whatever that Rut landed in Maine. His own admission, therefore, in regard to the *extent* of Norumbega alone crushes his argument.

But the case becomes still more clear when we remember what was before stated, that in Hakluyt's day the coast *north* as well as south of New England was still called Norumbega, which being the case, it is even *still less* reasonable to say that Rut visited Maine, because he touched at Norumbega. We could as well argue that a tourist must have "certainly" visited Maine because he returned to Europe "by the coasts" of the United States.

We might reasonably rest the argument here, but it is our duty to disabuse the reader's mind in regard to the correctness of Dr. Kohl's quotation, where he says that the Mary of Guilford "returned by the coasts of New Foundland, Cape Breton and Norumbega." This is not what Hakluyt says. Indeed, one feels considerable surprise after comparing the alleged language with that actually employed. Hakluyt does not say that they "returned by," but that they shaped their course "*towards*" the places in question. The writer has examined *all* the editions of Hakluyt, and the language is everywhere the same, with the exception that the first edition (1589), has "Arembec," which is the equivalent of Norumbega, Hakluyt simply says that after parting from the Sampson, the Mary of Guilford "shaped her course towards Cape Breton and the coasts of Arembec."

The full account stands as follows: "Sailing very far northwestward, one of the ships was cast away as it entered into a dangerous gulf, about the great opening between the north parts of New Foundland, and the country lately called by her majesty, Meta Incognita. Whereupon the other ship [Rut's] shaping her course towards Cape Breton and the coast of Arembec, and often times putting their men on land to search the state of those unknown regions."

From this it is clear that Dr. Kohl's quotation is incorrect, and also, that it is extremely doubtful whether Rut, after all, did more than to sail "towards" some part of the country of Arembec, or Norumbega. We might at first, indeed, take it for granted that the phrase "unknown regions," referred to the shores of Arembec; yet when the whole account is more carefully considered, especially in the light of Purchas's relation, not yet quoted, we incline to the belief that by those unknown regions is meant the unfrequented parts of Newfoundland adjoining Meta Incognita. Again, it must also be remembered, that if it *was* Arembec that they landed upon, we have no reason to infer that they landed in that particular section of Arembec now called Maine, since they would strike Arembec when they left Cape Breton, upon which they could coast for hundreds of miles before reaching Maine.

But we must now turn to the testimony of Purchas, which is later and more full. Hakluyt's account is meagre. He did not even know the name of both the ships, saying that one was the "Dominus Vobiscum." Purchas corrects this error, and gives a letter from Rut himself, who, however, makes no mention of Arembec or Norumbega. This letter was addressed to King Henry VIII, and was written at St. John's, Newfoundland, August 3, 1527.

He writes, that they first touched at Cape de Bas Harbor, where they staid ten days "ordering" the ship and fishing, after which they sailed *southward* to St. John's. Here they were on the third of August, and Rut says that as soon as they "have fished" they would be ready to depart northward toward Cape de Bas, and so along the coast, still northward, until they found their consort, from whence they would go, with all diligence, "to that island that we are commanded" (*Purchas*, vol III, p. 809).

What their commands were we have no difficulty in determining. The expedition was fitted out to seek a north-west passage. Neither of the versions of this voyage, therefore, afford ground for the statement that

Rut's expedition landed in Maine, which must be dismissed as a very great mistake. The coasting "towards" Cape Breton and Arembec appears from Rut's letter to have *ended*, before they reached that region, which *all* authorities at the time made Arembec include, and which is now known as New Brunswick and Nova Scotia. Rut says that they first coasted southward to St. John, Newfoundland, in search of the Sampson, and announces his intention to sail northward " along the coast till we may meet with our fellow."

Nor does it appear that Rut afterwards changed his mind, while we must also note the fact, communicated in his letter to the king, that before the separation from his consort it appears to have been arranged that, in case of such an event, they were to rendezvous at "Cape de Sper," and wait six weeks. The information of Purchas is later, and makes plain what Hakluyt left slightly obscure; while neither of these writers give any ground whatsoever, for the hasty assertion of Dr. Kohl, that Rut's company visited Maine, and were the first Englishmen who *certainly* set foot on the shores of Maine.

There is another point in this connection that demands attention. Dr. Kohl not only sends the Mary of Guilford to Maine, but he prolongs the voyage to the West Indies. First, it must be stated, that Herrera (*Dec.*, 11, lib. v, c. 3), tells us of an English vessel that appeared off Porto Rico, in 1519, the captain reporting, that, in company with another ship, they had been sent northward to find a passage to China. In the course of the voyage, this vessel, at a certain point, had been separated from her consort by a storm. They then sailed from this place, which was full of ice, and reached a warm sea, afterwards returning to the Bacalaos, "where they found fifty sail of vessels, Spanish, French and Portuguese, engaged in fishing, and that going on shore to communicate with the natives, the pilot, a native of Piedmont, was killed; that they proceeded afterwards along the coast to Chicora (North Carolina), and crossed over thence to the island of St. Juan (from Porto Rico). The Spaniards asking them what they sought in these islands, they said that they wished to explore in order to report to the king of England and to procure a load of Brazil wood." And Dr. Kohl, having already concluded that the Mary of Guilford ran down the American coast, infers that this was the ship described by Herrera, on account of a fancied resemblence.[1]

In order to harmonize the dates, Dr. Kohl, finding that Oviedo reports an English ship at Porto Rico in 1527, concludes that Herrera was in error in placing his date at 1519,

---

[1] Dr. Kohl here does little more than to repeat some speculations of Biddle (*Life of Cabot*, p. 274), by which the latter detracted from his valuable work.

and infers that both wrote about the same ship. His reason for this is threefold. First, the English authorities are silent in regard to an expedition. This is, however, no valid reason. The English authorities came near being silent in regard to Rut's; while there will never be an end of debate on the alleged voyage of Cabot in 1517. Second, the improbability that "all the alleged circumstances" of the two vessels should agree. To this it must be observed that "all" do *not* agree, as any one will see by a comparison. Third, Oviedo lived in Porto Rico in 1527. This appears more to the point, yet if such a story was told at that time, instead of 1519, why did he not say something about it?

The writer is not arguing now to show that Herrera was *not* in error, but simply to prove that Rut did not sail down the coast. If we were to accept Dr. Kohl's statement, that the expedition of Rut returned " by the coasts" of Norumbega, there might be more reason for the opinion, but as already shown, Hakluyt simply says that the Mary of Guilford sailed "towards" Cape Breton and Arembec, which is not the language that would have been employed to describe a voyage to the West Indies.

But something more must be said of the remarkable "coincidences," which are, however, shown most forcibly by the *lack* of coincidence. Among other things, we have to note that Herrera says that the captain of the vessel appearing in Porto Rico, reported *fifty* Spanish, French and Portuguese fishing vessels, while Rut mentions "eleven saile of Normans, and one Brittaine, and two Portugall barkes," And another notable "coincidence" is found in the fact that while Rut says that after losing his consort, he sailed into Cape de Bas, *this* Englishman reported that *he* sailed away from the region of ice into a warm ("boiling hot") sea, meaning the Gulf Stream, and *afterwards* returned to the Bacallaos, from whence they turned *again* to the south and reached the West Indies. Of course it is impossible to recognize in this account the action of Rut immediately after parting company with the Sampson. He went to no boiling hot sea, and yet we read about the argreement of *all* the alleged circumstances! From the account it even appears that Rut had been separated about a *month* from the Sampson, and yet had sailed no farther in the direction of the Gulf Stream than St. John's, Newfoundland, from whence he tells the king he would return *northward* to Cape de Bas. It certainly requires some power of imagination to find a parallel in the two cases.

Another difficulty stands in the way of Dr. Kohl's theory, which is found in the fact that there was not sufficient time for the Mary of Guilford to accomplish what is implied. We find from the date of De Prato's letter that on August 10, Rut was still at St. John's when it was his intention to sail north, find the Sampson, and prosecute the voyage of north-western discovery. This they were *bound to do;* and Rut speaks of an arrangement previously proposed to wait at Cape de Bas six weeks. But supposing they eventually violated every obligation to their companions and the king, how soon did they turn southward? How long were they exploring on the Maine coast and sailing leisurely to the West Indies? How long were they naturally detained at Porto Rico? "Some time," Dr. Kohl says. How long did it take them to reach St. Domingo? And when they were driven back from that place to Porto Rico again, how long did they stay trading in the port of St. German? Then, finally, how long a time must it have taken to sail back to England?

All these points are to be considered; and therefore when we learn from Hakluyt that the Mary of Guilford reached England at the *beginning of the following October,* the folly of supposing this vessel mentioned by Herrera was Rut's becomes quite apparent.

There is, however, one more point to be noticed in this connection. In the quotation from Herrera we read of a Piedmont pilot who was in the English ship that appeared in Porto Rico. And the question has been asked, Who was this man? Biddle and Kohl tell us that this was probably Verrazano. The assumption is supported by the following statements: First, that Verrazano instead of Thorne as Hakluyt asserts,[1] incited King Henry to send out the expedition; second, that Verrazano expressed a desire to perform another voyage.

It is also stated by Ramusio, though he does not give any proof, that this navigator

---

[1] Dr. Kohl effectually disposes of this view in opposing Biddle in the matter of Cabot's voyage of 1517. See *Dr. Kohl's Work.*

did go on a voyage after that of 1524. There was a *dateless* rumor abroad in Italy, coupled with the report of the alleged voyage, to the effect that Verrazano was killed by the savages and devoured in sight of his friends. On this foundation, after assuming that the English vessel described by Herrera was the Mary of Guilford, it is argued that Verrazano accompanied Rut, and met his fate as stated.

After this one might suppose that sufficient interest had been excited in connection with Maine. Yet Dr. Kohl, in speaking of the result of Rut's voyage, says (p. 288), among various other things: "The Mary of Guilford not only came in sight of the coast of Maine, but she also 'oftentimes put her men on land to search the state of these unknown regions,'" and that "it is not improbable, that it was on the occasion of this landing, that the celebrated French navigator, Verrazano, was killed by the Indians." Elsewhere (p. 284), we have Dr. Kohl's inference, that, "if a monument to the memory of this famous navigator should ever be contemplated, this would be the region in which it should be erected."

But having already demonstrated that there is not a line or word to show that John Rut, either probably or "certainly," landed on the coast of Maine, or even on any part of *Norumbega,* it is only necessary to say again, that this Piedmont pilot met his alleged death at "the Baccalaos," as Herrera states, and not in Maine. By Baccalaos, Herrera could not certainly have meant the coast of Maine. This place was where the English captain says he saw fifty sail of fishermen. The rendezvous of fishermen is indicated by Rut's letter which was at St. John's. It was therefore upon the island of Newfoundland that the pilot was killed, if killed at all; so that the suggestion of a monument to Verrazano for the Maine coast must be dismissed to the winds.

THE VOYAGE OF JOHN RUT. 61

As regards the real fate of Verrazano, we have other rumors than those given by Ramusio. According to Barcia, who wrote the well known *Annals of Florida*, one Juan the Florentin (see p. 8), was executed as a pirate, in the very year when Dr. Kohl imagines that he was devoured by the Indians of Maine.[1] This is the name by which Ver-

---

[1] Buckingham Smith, Esq., who has recently returned from Spain, informs me that during his investigations abroad he found a number of original documents that relate to the history of the Florentin, which confirm his own previous convictions. This person, supposed to be Verrazano, was captured at sea by Biscayans, taken to Cadiz, tried and convicted, and finally executed (October, 1527), while on his way to intercede for his life with the king. The place of his execution was at *El Pico*, the highest point in New Castile. Mr. Smith also suggests that much material will be found at Paris, whither it was carried from Spain by Napoleon. Mr. Stevens in his *Notes* (p. 36), says of Verrazano: "The Spaniards knew of his voyages [in 1524]. They had been watching for him and had caught him, and in 1527, hanged him." These strong statements somewhat spoil the tradition of Ramusio. It may be said that this disposition of Rut's voyage leaves the expedition mentioned by Herrera

razano was known in Spain, and it has long been considered probable that he was executed for plundering Cortez's ships.

---

unaccounted for. Yet that is not the fault of the writer. Besides it is hardly necessary to make any mystery out of the fact that an English ship appeared in the West Indies in 1527. Whoever looks closely at the account of Herrera, will see by the number of the crew, her armament and stores, that it could not have been a vessel, like the Mary of Guilford, fitted out for a quiet exploration of the north-west, while both her appointments and movements indicated a piratical character. Among the rest is the statement that they had a great abundance of wines and clothes.

The captain indeed professed to have a commission from the king of England, and offered to show it to one of the Spanish officers, who could not read English. Yet a pirate would not be likely to cruise without some kind of forged papers for an emergency.

THE VOYAGE OF ANDRÉ THEVET.

The only expedition mentioned in the whole volume that could possibly be fastened upon the territory of Maine is the alleged expedition of the monk, André Thevet, who claims to have visited this region in the year 1556.

In introducing this personage, Dr. Kohl feels that he is favoring the claims of an exceedingly poor authority, whose work he rates lower than that of the chart of Ribero. Most critics will place Thevet lower than the position in which Dr. Kohl leaves him.

Thevet professes to have run the American coast from Florida to the north of Newfoundland, and yet he does not find anything to say concerning the country between Florida and parallel 43° N.; a fact that awakens the liveliest suspicion at the outset, leading us to ask whether Thevet made the voyage at all. If this, however, is conceded, then comes the question in regard to the particular spot at which he touched. Dr. Kohl affirms that he landed in Maine, and assigns the mouth of the Penobscot as the place. Let us therefore examine the question.

Thevet writes as follows: "Having left Florida on the left hand with all its gulfs and capes, a river presents itself which is one of the finest rivers in the whole world, which we call Norumbega, and the aborigines Agoncy, which is marked on some sea charts as the Grand river" (*Cosmographie Universelle*, vol. II, 1008). He also says that some pilots would make him believe that "this country is the proper country of Canada. But I told them it was far from the truth, as this country lies in 43° N."

First, Thevet's knowledge of the location of Norumbega is defective. The principal facts in relation to this place are given in the discussion of the voyage of Rut (p. 44, *et seq.*), where it is shown that at the time of Thevet's alleged visit the term Norumbega was given by some to the whole coast as far down as Florida, though the name never had this extensive use *on the maps.* It is significant that the map of Gastaldi (1550), applies the name to the coast only as far south as the present border of New Brunswick. Thevet, however, says that Norumbega lay in the forty-third degree, which commences at Plymouth, Massachusetts, and ends at Rye Beach, New Hampshire. This shows that his ideas were very crude. Besides it is evident that the monk intends to represent his visit as made to a river in *that latitude*, so that the supposition that he went to Maine

---

[1] On folio 1024 of his *Cosmography*, Thevet gives the exact location of the river, which he sets down in longitude 311° 50′ and 42° 14′ latitude, which varies only three minutes from the position assigned to the Arnodie,

on a line north of 44°, does violence to his own representation.

. That Thevet may have *supposed* that he had reached the river in question, is not very unlikely, yet it has not been shown that such was actually the case. The *latitude* mentioned does not agree with the situation, the *name Agoncy* given as the Indian name of the Penobscot, is incorrect, while the *island*, supposed to be the Fox island, does not answer to the Fox island. The large Fox is, first of all, composed of two islands, with a deep passage through them described by Williamson (*History of Maine*, vol. I, p. 72), as averaging a mile wide, and instead of *eight*, it is encompassed by a great many islets, Williamson, with truth, making the number innumerable, or too numerous to mention.

---

while that place, according to his own statement, must have been full *one hundred and fifty miles* south of Norumbega, this being the distance the ship was blown, as will be seen by reference to the following pages.

The Long Island of Thevet's narrative seems to agree with the present Islesboro in its shape, but instead of *four* it is *ten* leagues in circumference. The "Green mountains," described as being near this place, Dr. Kohl suggests were the Camden hills, yet Ribero, 1527, puts the Green mountains (*Montana Verde*), close to the Hudson (San Antonio) river, while Mercator, three years after the date of Thevet's alleged voyage (1569), sets them far south in the same locality. Thevet says that this place was also near the "cape of the isles," which Dr. Kohl suggests may mean "Cape de Mucha isles." But these were generally put near the present Camden hills, though occasionally as far south as latitude 40°. Still it is very well known that the "Cape of the Isles" were at that day distinct from the Cape Muchas isles, the former being placed a very long way *north* of the Long Island, and answering to the Schoodic Point, which lies opposite the isle of Mount Desert. There is therefore little or nothing in the description that can be confidently applied; while islands in the shape of a man's arm, as Thevet puts it, are everywhere to be found.

No one has before this thought it worth while to introduce Thevet among the ancient worthies who visited the coast. His works have always been well known, but not highly esteemed. Dr. Kohl's remark (p. 419), that various writers have copied his description of Norumbega, must be taken *cum grano salis*. He indeed cites Wytfliet's *Ptolemaicæ Augmentum* (p. 97), yet that author simply borrows a few lines of general description, which he turns into Latin, and welds on to his own remarks, without the slightest recognition of Thevet or his work.

The facts as given by Dr. Kohl, even, do not inspire confidence in the assertion that Thevet visited Maine. The indications suggest a more southern point.

But Dr. Kohl does not exhaust the relation of Thevet in its bearings upon this subject, which is dismissed too soon, after giving so much as seemed to favor this theory. The succeeding portions of the narrative are very suggestive. These portions show that the monk was in great darkness himself, and poorly prepared to withstand the pilots, who told him that the place in question was the country of Canada, instead of Norumbega. But let us proceed to his narrative.

After reaching the river of Norumbega, and delaying five days, they set sail, and went out into the open sea to avoid the shallows and rips. He says, "We had not proceeded more than fifteen leagues before there came a contrary east wind, and the sea was so rough that we were near perishing; and finally the gale drove us some fifty leagues from that place to the mouth of the river Arnodie, situated between Judi (*Juvdi*) and the cape on the right, where we were compelled to enter half a league and drop anchor to escape the storm and the fury of the sea." Here they were hospitably received and obtained an abundance of both fresh and salt water fish, especially of salmon. Where " Arnodie " lay does not exactly appear; but supposing they were at the mouth of the Penobscot when they set out (of which, be it remembered, we have no proof), the fifteen leagues first sailed out into the open sea would only have carried them forty-five miles around to the outside of Mount Desert. Then came the eastern gale, which if it had driven them straight leeward, as was usually the case with the inferior vessels of those days, they would inevitably have gone to pieces upon the iron bound shores of Maine, before driving fifty miles from the point where the gale struck them. But, as appears to have been the case *from this narrative*, the wind allowed them to put the head of the ship off shore, and keep far enough out at sea to drift without touching the land for fifty leagues, or one hundred and fifty miles. In that case when they made a harbor, if the account relates to this coast at all, they must have come to land somewhere towards Boston bay.[1] This, however, places them in an awkward position to enter upon the course that follows. We read : "Leaving this river [Arnodie] and coasting straight along Baccalaos,[2] we journeyed and ploughed the sea, as far as the Isle Thevet and thence to the Isles of St. Croix, of the Bretons and the savages, to the head of Cape Breton."

And where, according to the monk, was Baccalaos? This place he distinctly says

---

[1] In giving the position of Arnodie on folio 1024, of his *Cosmography*, Thevet places it in 42° 11' N. If this is a true account of a genuine voyage, the cape may have been Cape Cod. But by Cape Cod Dr. Kohl understands Cape Arenas, which Thevet puts in latitude 38° N. His obscure language is as follows: *Laissant ceste riviere & Costoiant de droit fil de la part de Baccalaos*, f. 1009.

[2] Thevet here represents himself as sailing on the coast of Baccalaos.

was in 48° 30' N. The name was not applied to the New England coast, upon which he must have been sailing, if sailing at all, and, moreover, he elsewhere appropriates the whole region under the divisions of Norumbega, Angouleme and Acadie. The whole account shows too much unacquaintance with the places in question to allow us to place him definitely on any part of the coast of Maine.

Thevet is a notoriously poor authority, and adds a mendacious spirit to an incredulous mind. His works will everywhere justify the sharpest criticism, and when we find him saying that his countrymen had taken possession of this region, and built a fort, long before his own arrival, we are forced to put the assertion with that to the effect that the neighboring region to the north was discovered by the Bretons in 1504, and that French pilots had a share in the discovery of South America.

Thevet certainly could have had no real knowledge of the place he endeavors to describe. Elsewhere we find him speaking of the gulf full of islands that lies between Angouleme and Acadie, whereas that gulf, the present Bay of Fundy, is not so distinguished. Thevet had no acquaintance with the localities, since he had in mind the islands of the Maine coast, while Angouleme and Acadie are represented by the modern New Brunswick and Nova Scotia, Angouleme terminating at the mouth of the St. Croix river. Nor can we fail to notice that he both ambitiously manages to have an island called after his name, and pretends to have named Angouleme himself in honor of his birthplace; but it is the simple truth, that the name was applied by others long before.

Thus far we have gone on showing that, in case this voyage was really made along the New England coast, we have no authority for believing that he landed in Maine. But it is now time to consider whether he made the voyage at all. His bungling and contradictory narrative would be sufficient to banish him from the coast, but the sketches of his biographers seem to do more. Dr. Kohl indeed writes (p. 416), that he "appears to have sailed along the coast of North and South America," and says, "see upon this, Jöcher, *Gelehrten Lexicon*, vol. IV, p. 1130." But nothing more is there conveyed than that he returned from Brazil in the course of a year. Dr. Kohl says that Thevet *seems* to have sailed these coasts, from language used in his *Singularities of Antarctic France*, a work that the monk had the assurance so to style at a time when the total strength of France in South America was eighty men confined on a rock in the harbor of Rio Janeiro.[1] Yet Dr. Kohl, or any one else, would not

---

[1] See *Southey's Brazil*, vol. I, p. 172.

wish to quote the language referred to as proof. On this point his biography is pretty conclusive. Jöcher's work was published in 1751. Yet in *Biographie Universelle*,[1] (1826-27), we find that Thevet left Havre, France, July 12, 1555, and reached Rio Janeiro on the 10th or 14th of the following November. It is related that he "fell sick almost as soon as he touched the land, and had only recovered when he reembarked for France, January 31, 1556, without having been able to examine Brazil, of which he nevertheless gave a very circumstantial account." Therefore it was with good reason that Lery began his work, *Navigationis Braziliam* (1586), with a refutation of the errors and frauds (*errores ac fraudes*) of Thevet, who had still poorer grounds for describing Mexico, Florida and the country beyond latitude 42° N., where

---

[1] See article on Thevet, Div. I, vol. 45, and Sketch of Villegagnon, vol. XLIX.

he did not go, as his own miserable account and the silence of his biographers (La Roquette and Weiss) clearly prove.

Dr. Kohl himself confesses (p. 419), that, "the other rivers, the capes, and islands of Maine and Nova Scotia, which he incidently mentions, are not easily identified, and his observations on them are not of any value." Indeed they cannot be identified at all, even where they are not incidentally but specifically mentioned, as they are inextricably jumbled up with fabulous matters, such as the Isle of Demons, and the Two Chateaux (which appears to be the beginning of the fabulous *city* of Norumbega?),[1] the Exiled Woman, and the Adventures of the Nestorian Bishop.

The most reasonable view, therefore, is that Thevet never made the voyage in question, but constructed his story from maps and

---

[1] See *Lescarbot*, by Errondelle, p. 46.

the relations of others. If the ship in which he took passage thus went out of her course, we should expect to find some proof of it in Thevet's biography. Again we see that it is unreasonable. In order to reach *Florida* (not to say Mexico), it would be necessary to sail westward across the South Atlantic about *forty-five degrees* out of the direct course. And after reaching Florida they are represented as penetrating towards the neighborhood of Greenland, where for twenty days (in midsummer?), they were tormented by the frosts, after which they sailed, we know not where. The object of this alleged voyage is not stated, nor have we any particulars of its beginning or termination, though if it had really been made there would have been no end to the relation of Thevet's adventures. But Thevet himself is almost *silent*. On no page of his ponderous works can the investigator show proof of his personal contact with the North American coast; he tells us nothing of value which others had not told before. The fresh, glowing recital, that flows from a mind kindling with the recollections of a new world, is wanting. In a word, *this relation of Thevet appears to be a fraud.*

Such is the result of some examination of Dr. Kohl's work, so far as it bears directly upon the history of Maine, to whose annals it adds so little. During the long period intervening between the voyages of the Northmen and the charter of Gilbert, he fails to show a single European actually stepping upon the Maine shore. That such there were we cannot doubt, yet they came and went, leaving scarcely more than footprints, hastily pressed on the shining sand. And thus to-day we enter the great libraries of the old world, search the dusty alcoves of feudal homes, and delve amid the mouldy archives of ancient sea-port towns, vainly endeavoring to illustrate with some fragment of narrative, the rude, but still invaluable, partisan map we bear. In connection with the period referred to, Dr. Kohl has not yet shown *one authentic paragraph* to shed light upon the history of that romantic coast, which stretches in all its wild, unequaled beauty, from the Piscataqua to the St. Croix. Patient industry may in the future meet with its reward; yet whoever looks for fresh light on the history of early Maine, must not only learn to labor but to *wait*.

THE DISCOVERY OF MASSACHUSETTS BAY.

In the foregoing papers the effort has been made to assign several of the alleged Maine voyages of Dr. Kohl to their proper place, and to exhibit something of the process by which the narratives were drawn into a wrong connection. It now remains, therefore, in closing, to give a single example illustrating the faults of omission.

That there should be anything to say on this point should not be considered very remarkable. Yet much time, talent, and money, has been expended to make the work as complete as possible, and every class of allusion that came in the way has been garnered up and brought to lend an interest to the coast of Maine. The obscurest reference known to the author has been utilized and minutely dwelt upon for the purpose of showing its relation to a single spot on the New England coast. The omission referred to is at least noticeable, especially as the means of information in this case were open to all.

It is but just, however, to add that in this instance Dr. Kohl finds himself in the company of not only every New England, but even every national writer, that has undertaken to treat, either little or much, of the early voyages to America. All of these writers fail to notice the voyage which, perhaps, carried the navigator along the coast of Maine, while it certainly was extended to Massachusetts Bay, and formed its first well authenticated rediscovery. Even Mr. Palfrey in his cautiously written narrative of early voyages along the New England coast, does not allude to this occurrence in the slightest way, even though he enumerates every expedition known to him that could possibly enhance the interest of his history of New England.

But before speaking of the voyage in question, let us first notice some things by which it was preceded.

If the generally received interpretation of the Icelandic Sagas is correct, the Northmen of the eleventh century must be viewed as the *original* European discoverers of Massachusetts bay. To this honor they, indeed, make no claim, yet their simple narratives describe such a place, and reveal the fact that they were familiar with the entire locality around which Cape Cod throws its sheltering arm. Thorvald Ericson, in the spring of 1004, became acquainted with Cape Cod, where he broke the keel of his vessel, and afterwards crossed to Plymouth and sailed along the coast towards Boston, where he lost his life.

In the year 1008, Thorhall the Hunter, who was attached to the expedition of Thorfinn Karlsefne, attempted to sail around Cape Cod and enter Massachusetts bay, but failed, and was driven out to sea by a storm.

In the year 1009, Karlsefne himself went around Cape Cod and sailed along the coast until, off Boston, he raised the Blue Hills, when he returned to the settlement in Rhode Island, appearing unwilling to venture up the coast of New Hampshire and Maine, on account of the Unipeds, or *one-footed men*, fabled to live there; in which we trace the equivalent, if not the origin of the Isle of Demons, in modern times a terror to the French and Spanish sailors, who declared that they often distinctly heard terrible cries and yells of the fiends.

With Karlsefne's voyage, the connection of the Northmen with the bay in question comes to an end, so far as the record goes.

That the Northmen were familiar with this bay, is also apparent from the map drawn by Sigardus Stephanius in 1570, and given in Torfæus's *Gronlandia Antiqua*. On this map we have the *Promontorium Vinlandiæ*, answering to Cape Cod, and very distinctly laid down with a bay within, answering well enough to Massachusetts bay. The latitude is placed too far north, yet an error of this sort might have been expected at a time when the draughtsman had no scientific data for his guidance. The northern end of the cape he places in 56° North, yet this part of the map is no more crude than the Greenland section. On the whole, considering the means which Stephanius had at hand for his work, he was quite successful. Especially does this appear when we compare this performance with later maps.

Dr. Kohl, while admitting the value of the map, felt troubled because the cape is represented on so large a scale, and apologizes for this, on the ground that the place made a large figure in the accounts of the voyages, and therefore led the draughtsman to give it this prominence in his sketch. And this remark should doubtless have a certain weight, though it is perhaps, on the whole, not needed, as will appear from the fact that the Cape .Cod of to-day is not the Cape Cod of the eleventh century. This region has undergone very extensive changes,[1] and does not present the area that it once

---

[1] The author in his work on *Pre-Columbian Discovery* (p. 29), has called attention to this fact, showing from the Sagas, and from recent investigations, that a large island and a piece of land formerly lay off the eastern shore of Cape Cod, where now is an open sea, this view having the approval of Prof. Agassiz, who considers the evidence as conclusive as any geological evidence could well be. Mr. John Doane, born near what Gosnold named Point Care, testified in 1864, that "his father and grandfather, in fact all his ancestors from the first settlement, owned the land and the meadows between Isle Nauset and the main. He says that, *within* his recollection, Point Care has worn away *about half a mile*. When his grandfather was a boy, Point Care extended much farther

filled. In Gosnold's time the island and part of the headland called Point Gilbert remained; though in 1680, the Labadist

---

into the ocean than it did when he was young. These are not vague and uncertain recollections. Mr. Doane points to monuments, and the exact distance that the ocean has encroached on the land within his recollection can be ascertained. He states that fifty years ago a beach extended from the present entrance of Nauset harbor, half a mile north, where the entrance was. Within this beach his father owned ten acres of salt meadows, on which, he for several years assisted him in cutting and raking the hay. Now where that beach was there are three or four fathoms of water, and where the meadows were is a sand bar on which the waves continually break, and make Nauset harbor difficult of access. Within his memory, the north beach connected with Eastham shore, has extended south one mile, and the whole beach has moved inward about its width, say one fourth of a mile." Mr. Doane also testifies that in the middle of Isle Nauset there was a rocky piece of land known as Slut's Bush, and that he had formerly picked berries there. This spot now lies some distance from shore in deep water, where the fisherman often tangles his lines among the roots of old trees that still remain, multitudes of which have come ashore during heavy gales. Furthermore, "Beyond Slut's Bush, about three miles from the shore, there is a similar ledge called

Brethren, according to the first volume of the Long Island Historical Society (p. 377), say: "Cape Cod is a clean coast, where

Beriah's ledge, probably formed in precisely the same manner as Slut's Bush is known to have been formed."

Mr. Otis also says: "We have historical and circumstantial evidence, that Point Gilbert existed in 1602; it united with the main land at James head near Chatham lights. From James head, on its south shore, it extended nine miles on an east by south course to its eastern terminus, afterwards known as Webb's island, situate where Crabb's ledge now is. Cape Care was worn away by the gradual abrasion of the waves. Over Point Gilbert the sea, during a violent gale, swept, carrying away long sections in a single day." He adds, Morse states [*Univer. Geog.*, I, 317, ed., 1793], "that Webb's island at one time contained fifteen acres of rocky land covered with wood, from which the early inhabitants of Nantucket procured fuel. The process which has been described as having occurred at Slut's Bush ledge also occurred at Crabb and island ledges; the stumps and roots of trees were carried down by the superincumbent rocks. Mr. Joshua Y. Bearse, who resided many years at Manamoit point, and has all his life been familiar with the shoals and ledges near Chatham, informs me that it is very difficult to obtain an anchor lost near either of these ledges; the sweeps used catch against the rocks and stumps at the bottom; that in repeated instances he has pulled up there are no islands, rocks or banks." They also add what was not at all true half a century before, not wholly true at the time they wrote, namely: " therefore all such laid

---

stumps of trees from the bottom where the water is four fathoms deep. He also states that after the violent gale in 1851, during which the sea broke over Nauset beach, * * sweeping away banks of earth twenty feet high, cutting channels therein five fathoms deep, moving the sea to its very bottom, and tearing up old stumps which had been there more than a century. Mr. Bearse states that more than one hundred of these drifted during that gale to the shore at Manamoit beach; and that he picked them up for fuel. A part of these stumps bore the mark of the axe, but the greater part were broken or rotted off." *Mass. Hist. and Gen. Register*, 1864, p. 43.

The foregoing shows what has been wrought by the ravages of the sea during the last two and a half centuries, and gives some ground for inference in regard to what must have been effected by the same agent between the time of the Northmen and the voyage of Gosnold. The whole region is composed of what the geologist calls drift, or sand and gravel, easily carried away by the waves. Everything goes to prove that the sea around Cape Cod was once nearly filled up by this formation. Nantucket and Martha's Vineyard were once connected, and may have been a part of the system which included the islands that rose above the sea where the shoals of Georges now

down on the charts of the great reef of Malebarre and otherwise is false." The old maps,[1] though made on poor information, are nevertheless right, so far as they go in indi-

---

appear. Point Gilbert and other outlying portions of the land that have more recently disappeared had *nuclei* composed of rock and clay which enabled them to resist the force of the waves for a much longer period than the parts not thus protected. We see an illustration of the same thing, at Highland Light to-day, where the well known Clay Pounds stand forth to buttress the sandy cliffs rapidly washing away, and which will one day disappear, and leave a point of land extending into the sea.

It may be mentioned in this connection, that the truth of Verazzano's relation has been questioned, because he passes Cape Cod without recognizing its remarkable features, or noticing the shoals of Georges. If the foregoing facts had been borne in mind, the objection would not probably have been urged, as we do not know that any shoals were in existence at that place in 1524. This is very likely the well known history of the famous Goodwin Sands repeated in America. On the whole, therefore, the old map of Stephanius needs hardly to be apologized for, on account of the large area which it gives to the promontory of Vinland, or Cape Cod.

[1] At the present time the material being taken by the sea from Cape Cod is said to be transported to the northward, where a shoal is now forming.

cating the islands and the shoals east of Cape Cod which have been scoured away. Visscher's map is of particular interest in this connection.

At what time Cape Cod appears in the cartology of the seventeenth century, it would perhaps be difficult to determine. So remarkable a region should, on all just principles, have made some figure in the French, Spanish and Portuguese maps of the previous century, yet we are left in doubt whether Cape St. Mary, on Ruscelli's map of 1561, and Cape *de Arenas*, found on earlier maps, really refer to Cape Cod or not.

That this region was often coasted by navigators of different nations, there can of course be no doubt, yet it is very plumply declared in Folsom's *History of Saco and Biddeford* (p. 9), that "that the discovery of New England may justly be ascribed to Bartholomew Gosnold, an enterprising and intelligent navigator, who, in the year 1602, performed a voyage to this part of North America, before unknown to the civilized world."

Coming down to a more recent date, we find Barry, in his *History of Massachusetts* (p. 9), declaring that "the first English voyage resulted in the *discovery* of Massachusetts." This is supplemented by a note on the same page, where it is said, " The shores of Massachusetts may have been, and doubtless were, seen before this time; but the discovery of Gosnold is the first we are able to authenticate by that species of evidence which rises above mere conjecture or strong probability." That this is an error will shortly appear.

Mr. Palfrey is more cautious, and after alluding to the Northmen, to Madoc, the Zeni, Cortereal, Skolnus, the Cabots, Verazzano, Gomez, and Gilbert, he properly mentions Gosnold, Brereton, and three others, as " the first Englishmen known to have set foot upon the soil of Massachusetts." (*History of New England*, p. 71). Mr. Drake, however, in his painstaking *History of Boston* (p. 12), says, with less precision, that Gosnold was "the first of any nation who had reached any part of the United States, except Verrazani." Dr. Kohl and the Maine writers are therefore no worse off than the historians of Massachusetts.

But it is now time to speak of the voyage alluded to at the outset as overlooked by all American writers. The person to whom we are indebted for this voyage was Jean Allfonsce of Saintonge, who in the year 1542, went out to Canada as the pilot of Roberval's expedition, and who mentions his voyage to the southward in a work which he composed with the aid of an assistant, and left substantially finished at his death. The original manuscript is now in the Imperial Library at Paris. Several professed copies of this work have appeared in print, yet they are represented as imperfect abstracts. One of these, a quarto volume, appeared in 1550, under the title of *The Adventurous Voyages of Captain Jan Alfonce Saintongeois.* A second edition appeared in 1578, and a third is mentioned of 1598.

M. Davezac, in his brief article on Allfonsce, which will be given before closing the subject, says that Margry intended to include it in his volume then (1857) under preparation. It does not, however, appear in his *Navigations Francaises* (1867) except in extracts. And among these will be found the following:

" *Ces terres tiennent à la Tartarie, et pense que ce se soit le bout de l'Asie selon la rondeur du monde. Et pour ce il seroit bon avoir ung navire petit de soixante et dix tonneaux pour descouvrir la coste de la Fleuride, car j'ay esté à une baye jusques à 42 degrés, entre Norembegue et la Fleuride, mais n'ay pas veu du tout le fond et ne sçay pas s'il passe plus avant.*" (*Navigations Françaises et La Révolution Maritime* Du XIVᵉ au XVIᵉ *Siècle*, p. 323, ed. 1867).[1]

This rendered into English stands as follows:

"These lands reach to Tartary, and, I think that it is the end of Asia, according to the roundness of the world. And for this purpose it would be well to have a small vessel of seventy tons in order to discover the coast of Florida, for I have been at a bay as far as forty-two degrees, between Norumbega and Florida, but I have not seen the end, and I do not know whether it extends any farther."

Margry quotes this passage, however, with reference not to shedding light upon Massachusetts history, but to illustrate Allfonsce's

---

[1] I have to acknowledge my obligations to J. Carson Brevoort, Esq., president of the Long Island Historical Society, for pointing out this extract in Margry, referring to the voyage of Allfonsce, likewise for frequent suggestions,

belief of a north-west passage to India, as the French captain also thought that the Saguenay river might likewise lead to the Pacific or to Cathay. Margry did not perceive the really great point of interest in connection with the extract, as his studies do not lead him to investigate such points of local history. Nevertheless we see very clearly that Allfonsce, in the voyage alluded to, discovered Massachusetts bay, which lies in the latitude mentioned. This navigator followed a seafaring life for many years, and was a most experienced and careful pilot, whose computations could be depended upon. Such was the value of his services, that they were coveted by the Portuguese, under whose flag he sailed for a time, which has led historical students of that nation to claim him as a fellow countryman. Allfonsce sailed down

---

and the use of most valuable, and otherwise inaccessible, works, which the author has had occasion to consult from time to time.

the coast past Nova Scotia, and then, perhaps, shaped his course westward to the shores of Maine. The latter is, at *present*, conjecture, for he may have pursued a southward course on leaving Nova Scotia, as the Northmen and many others did, and next sighted Cape Cod, or the coast of New Hampshire. That he discovered Cape Cod, must be regarded as certain, and likewise the opposite cape, now called Cape Ann; otherwise he could not have known that the water in question was a bay. Whether he landed or not, he does not say, yet this is very probable. Still he distinctly declares that he did not sail to the end of it, and therefore was unable to say whether it extended through the continent to India or not.

Until some earlier claimant is brought forward, to Jean Allfonsce must be awarded the modern discovery of Massachusetts bay, hitherto unanimously assigned to Bartholomew Gosnold in his voyage of 1602. The proof is not founded upon anything shadowy or doubtful, but is scientific and circumstantial.

That the students of Massachusetts history should have overlooked the account of this voyage, is noticeable from the fact that for more than two centuries and a half they could have read the account in English; obscurely packed away within the dusky tomes of Hakluyt, but surely there, in the end of the article headed:

" Here followeth the course from *Belle Isle, Carpont,* and the *Grand Bay* in *Newfoundland* vp the riuer of *Canada* for the space of 230 leagues, obserued by *John Alphonse* of *Xanctoigne,* chiefe Pilote to *Monsieur Roberual,* 1542."

The language of Hakluyt runs as follows:

These landes lye ouer against Tartarie, and I doubt not but that they stretch toward Asia, according to the roundnesse of the world. And therefore it were good to haue a small shippe of

70 tunnes to diſcouer the coaſt of New France on the backe ſide of Florida: for I haue bene at a Bay as farre as 42 degrees betweene Norumbega and Florida, and I haue not ſearched the ende, and I know not whether it paſſe through. (*Hakluyt*, vol. III, p. 239, ed. 1600).

This narrative of Jean Allfonsce was, perhaps, extracted by Hakluyt from one of the mutilated versions of his work already alluded to, and was placed thus early within the reach of English-reading students, by whom it has uniformly been overlooked, which shows how little Hakluyt's work is really read.[1]

It will be perceived by a comparison of Hakluyt's version with the copy made from the

---

[1] The same remark also applies to Purchas. So long ago as the date of the publication of Biddle's *Cabot*, that author essayed, by a reference to Purchas, to stop the complaints of such men as Dr. Lardner and the Edinburgh encyclopædists, who lamented that nothing was known of the voyage of John Rut (1527), except what was told in Hakluyt. Yet, so far as that point was concerned, Biddle used his ink very much in vain, since a

original manuscript, that the Englishman is very faulty, as Allfonsce says nothing about "the coast of New France on the back side of Florida," a remark having no applicability to the case.¹

---

short time ago a well known, industrious, and highly respectable New England writer, treated the subject of Rut's voyage in the utter unconsciousness of the fact that Purchas had given a later and more correct version. See *ante*, p. 50.

¹ If we had the whole work of Allfonsce at hand with which to compare the extract given by Hakluyt, we should probably find many errors of the same kind. Margry, in his *Navigations Françaises* (p. 326), exhibits one of a most ridiculous character. Hakluyt writes on the same page already quoted from (239) as follows:

"By the nature of the climate the lands toward Hochelaga are still better and better, and more fruitfull. And this land is fit for Figges and Peares. And I thinke that golde and siluer will be found here, according as the people of the countrey say."

Here Hakluyt mangles Allfonsce's words so as to make him say that *figs* grew in Canada, and changes Peru (*Perou*) into *pears*; whereas Allfonsce, as Margry testifies, simply meant to say that the land of the "Fig Tree" extended northward to this region. By the Fig Tree was meant a *cape of Yucatan*. It will therefore be seen

Dr. Kohl refers to Jean Allfonsce in his work (p. 344), in connection with the voyages of Cartier, and says that Hakluyt gives "excellent sailing directions for the gulf and river of St. Lawrence made by this navigator," all the while unconscious of the fact that he actually gave a notice of a voyage down the New England coast to Massachusetts bay, worth infinitely more for his purpose than any reference that he has given. Indeed, this is the only positive account, in the original statement, that we now know of a

---

that Hakluyt's version cannot be trusted at all, and that it is very likely that with these "excellent sailing directions," as Dr. Kohl styles them, the sailor would be liable to come to grief. The original work, in the Imperial Library at Paris, no doubt deserves the commendation. M. Davezac says that he has seen a perfect copy made by Margry with his own hand, which at one time the latter intended to publish in full. The original language of Allfonsce stands thus: "*Les terres allant vers Hochelaga sont de beaucoup meilleures et plus chauldes que celles de Canada et tient cette terre de Hochelaga au Figuier et au Perou, en laquelle abonde or et argent.*"

voyage to any particular spot on the New
England coast during that long period intervening between the days of the Northmen
and the date of the charter of Gilbert, a
period that Dr. Kohl has vainly endeavored
to make interesting in connection with the
coast of Maine. After reciting *unreal* visits
to the coast of Maine by the Northmen, John
Rut, Verrazano,[1] Thevet and others, it is
surprising to find Jean Allfonsce left out of
the account.[2] This we must conclude was

---

[1] The reference here is, of course, to the alleged visit
of Verrazano in 1527, in company with Rut, at a time
when the Florentin had probably been executed. Conceding, as the author is free to, the voyage made by that
navigator on the American coast, in 1524, we still know
nothing of the particular regions seen after leaving the
harbor of New York, or, perhaps, I should add, the
harbor of Newport also. The mention of *islands* would
seem to indicate an acquaintance with the Maine coast
derived either from personal observation or the relations
of others.

[2] The reference to the voyage of Maldonado is in
general terms, like the statement of the voyage of Cabot
and others along the American coast. Dr. Kohl remarks:

because he was unacquainted with his achievment.

It would be very gratifying if we were able to fix the precise date of this voyage, yet this is impossible. Allfonsce mentions the subject in the most modest manner, little dreaming that his excursion down the coast was of any consequence at all, unless, indeed, the bay mentioned should prove to be an opening through the continent. His general account of this region in which his voyage is

---

"The principal account of this voyage is given by Garcilaso de la Vega, who says that Maldonado, in 1540, having explored the coast of the Gulf of Mexico for his absent chief without success, extended his search in 1541, with his companion, Gomez Arias, along the eastern coast as far as the country of Bacallaos" (p. 410). He also says: "That this expedition in 1541, 'as far as the Bacallaos,' must have involved a thorough search of our coast, may also be inferred from the circumstance, that Maldonado, in 1542–1543, returned directly to the gulf, visiting again our east coast" (p. 410). He would, therefore, have us believe that Maldonado went to Maine, yet of this we have no account, nor do we know what region is meant by the writer.

mentioned, was written in 1542, though we do not know in what month. And since we do not hear anything of a voyage prior to this, made as the pilot of Roberval, we naturally ask if it was made in the summer of this year.

We find that the expedition left Rochelle April 16, 1542, and arrived at St. John's, Newfoundland, June 8th, where they remained until the close of the month before proceeding to Quebec. Ten or twelve days would have been ample for such an excursion with one of the vessels, yet it is not mentioned, though the next year they made an effort to explore the Saguenay. It is also told, though not in the relation of Hakluyt, which gives the account of Roberval's expedition, that Allfonsce was sent to seek a north-west passage. Charlevoix testifies on this point, and Father Leclerc mentions it with equal explicitness. Says the latter, as quoted by Margry (*Navigations Françaises*, p.

321). "The Sire Roberval writes that he undertook some considerable voyages to the Saguenay, and several other rivers. It was he who sent Allfonsce, a very expert pilot (*pilote trés-expert*) of Saintonge, to Labrador in order to find a passage to the East Indies, as was hoped. But not being able to carry out his design, on account of the mountains of ice that stopped his passage, he was obliged to return to M. de Roberval with only this advantage, of having discovered the passage which is between the isle of the New-land and the great Land of the North by the 52d degree."

This northern voyage is not mentioned by Hakluyt, though he speaks of the Saguenay expedition. When, therefore, did this expedition to the north of Labrador take place? This question is asked, for the reason that it has a bearing upon the main point being considered, namely, the voyage to Massachusetts bay.

Now we may regard it as certain that Roberval did not send Allfonsce on this voyage at a time when he had but one vessel left, for he would need a ship for his own safety; and yet after the autumn of 1542 he was left with a single ship, as at that time he dispatched two of his three ships to France. Therefore it follows, that the voyage in search of a passage beyond Labrador was made in the summer of 1542, when three ships were ready for employment. This being so, it is reasonable to infer that, failing in his trip around Labrador, Jean Allfonsce may then, if not while the expedition delayed at St. John's, in June, have run down the coast to latitude forty-two, where he found himself at last locked within the outreaching capes that stand on either side of the mouth of Massachusetts bay.

Here then we have *two* occasions during the summer of 1542, when he might easily have made the voyage; and since we hear of no other voyage made by him to the northern part of this continent, it is reasonable to infer that the discovery was made in the year alluded to.

Why he did not push on to the bottom of the bay is not told. He would probably have done so, however, if some exigency had not prevented, as was the case with Verrazano, when, in 1524, he was driven away by the violence of the wind from the bay of New York.

At all events it is certain that this voyage was made during some visit to the region of the St. Lawrence, and that up to the year 1542 he had never run the American coast beyond latitude 42° N.

The supposition that he had sailed to the north prior to his voyage with Roberval is also, at the same time, perfectly reasonable, and the fact no such voyage is mentioned is nothing whatever against the performance. We learn from Melin Saint-Gelais that Allfonsce followed the sea for forty-one years;[1] and since his death took place in 1549, at the least we have a period of thirty-four years devoted to maritime life prior to 1542. Nevertheless, in the absence of positive proof, we may be allowed to assign the summer of 1542 as the date of the discovery of Massachusetts bay.

Of the general actions of Allfonsce while in the expedition of Roberval, we have no account, though Hakluyt (vol. III, p. 240, ed. 1600), says : " There is a pardon to be seene for the pardoning of *Monsieur de saine terre*, Lieutenant of the sayd *Monsieur de Roberual* giuen in *Canada* in presence of the sayde *Iohn Alphonse*."

Of the events in the life of Jean Allfonsce we know but little, nor is this so remarkable, considering the fact that he lived in an age when one of his patrons, the Prince Pen-

---

[1] Davezac makes the time forty-eight years.

tagruel, was largely lost to sight, and is now, even, scarcely remembered, except by antiquarians. The date of his birth is not given, though we learn the place of his nativity from the wretched edition of his *Hydrography*, published in 1559. Indeed, Margry remarks (*Navigations Françaises*, p. 226), that this is the only thing of value in the book, which, otherwise, might just as well have never been printed. The village of Saintonge, in the canton of Cognac, in France, enjoys the honor, though Portuguese writers have claimed him for their nation, in whose ships he served for a time in voyages to Brazil.

In 1528, we find him in a prison of Poitiers, where he was confined by royal orders, because, as alleged, he presumed to carry himself with as much haughtiness as the king. His death must have taken place some time between 1547 and 1549.

The *Hydrography* of Allfonsce also shows the most convincing proofs of his origin. In the course of his work, he reveals the national pride by extolling beautiful France above all the countries of the earth, representing that country as the home of all elegance and greatness, and as specially renowned for science, literature, enterprise, commerce and art.

His eulogist, Melin Saint-Gelais,[1] was also a Frenchman, and the friend of Marot and Rabelais. His poem of fourteen lines, in praise of the renowned pilot, stands in the original, and very imperfect, abridgement of his work.

---

[1] *Melin de Saint-Gelais* was the son of the bishop of Angouleme, a man of some distinction both as a poet and an ecclesiastic. The date of his birth is not given, though it is stated that he was educated at Padua and Poitiers, and became an ecclesiastic. He cultivated literature to a large extent, and joined Rabelais in his opposition to the poet Ronsard at the court of King Henry II of France. Eventually his feelings changed, and he became a warmly attached friend to Ronsard. Saint-Gelais wrote both in Latin and French, and is known as the author of elegies, satires, epigrams, sonnets and epistles. He died in 1559.

The high character of Jean Allfonsce as a pilot and a hydrographer is conceded; and, while his works are not free from faults, it is clear that he was conversant with the nautical knowledge of his times, and that he was fully abreast of the very best pilots as respects all things connected with his profession.

As already intimated, he was a man of lofty spirit, and, while ardently attached to his native land, he did not fear to compare the government of China with that to which he was subject, and to declare that, in respect to its power to confer happiness, it was not behind the institutions of France; an opinion that leads his sincere admirer and appreciative critic, Pierre Margry, to suggest that he had seen Utopia. But perhaps M. Margry is a *monarchist*.

Had Allfonsce lived in our own day, he would have been an ardent assertor of the rights of the people against the claims of the crown; and, for ought we know, his visit to the prison of Poitiers may have been occasioned as much by the inflexibility of his principles as by the haughtiness of his spirit.

At all events it appears that Jean Allfonsce was in advance of the people of his nation, and that he openly declared himself in favor of an aristocratic republic like that of Venice in the grand old days when her free senators sat in princely state, and sent forth stern decrees from their lordly hall. Nor is it altogether an unhappy circumstance that the first recorded visit to the shores of liberty-loving Massachusetts should have been made by a mariner of this lofty stamp, and a pilot of the Prince Pentagruel.

Whether the course of Jean Allfonsce carried him to the coast of Maine we cannot say, yet this is altogether very likely. But if so, we at present have no knowledge of the fact, and thus Maine is left again without the coveted mention. Yet light may come.

We have now, in closing, to give a notice of Jean Allfonsce in connection with the unworthy abridgments of his work, an account of which will nevertheless prove both of interest and value to bibliographers. Probably not a single copy of either of the works mentioned has found its way to America. M. Margry, it appears, has not yet carried into execution his plan by which, as M. Davezac intimates in the following article, the work of Allfonsce was to appear entire. What he has given is, nevertheless, far more valuable than anything produced before.

The article referred to by M. Davezac, appears in *Bulletin du Geographie*, 1857, tome II, p. 317. We give it entire.

JEAN ALLFONSCE DE SAINTONGE.

"It has occurred more than once to the Portuguese nation to claim historically as its own those men whom the exclusive and jealous policy of this people had formerly tried to retain or call into its service, on account of the experience they had acquired in voyages to foreign lands. This, it seems to us, has been the case with the Spaniard, *Jean Diaz de Solis*, of Asturian origin, and declared a native of Lebrija, even by those who had the means of becoming the best informed.

"Thus it has been with the Frenchman, Jean Allefonsce (thus he wrote his name) de Saintonge, the excellent pilot whom Roberval had with him in his expedition to Canada, which left Rochelle April 16, 1542. and was brought back to France two years afterwards by Jacques Cartier.[1] Hakluyt

---

[1] This hardly gives a right view of the case. Roberval's expedition was brought back by Cartier, and by the knight himself. Cartier's expedition was a *part* of Roberval's which was dispatched the year before, as Roberval was not then ready to sail himself. Cartier was second in command, and in June, of 1542, he was returning with his ships to France from Canada, where he had passed a winter, and met Roberval in the harbor

has preserved ' An excellent Ruttier showing the course from Bell-Isle, Carpont and the Grand Bay up the river of Canada for the space of 230 leagues, observed by John Alphonse, of Xanctoigne, chiefe pilote to Monsieure Roberval, 1542.'

---

of St. John's, Newfoundland, and endeavored to persuade him to return to France, on account of the dangers and the hopelessness of the expedition. Failing in this, he ingloriously stole out of the harbor in the night, and sailed for France. Roberval, on the contrary, pushed forward about the close of the month up the St. Lawrence and wintered at Quebec, returning to France with his last remaining ship in the autumn of 1544. It is told that, in 1547, he attempted another expedition, and perished by shipwreck with all his company.

This is the way Hakluyt puts it, but other accounts make it appear that Cartier came out in 1543, and in 1544 took back to France some remnant of his expedition. Mr. Shea observes in his *Charlevoix* (vol I, p. 129), that his own author, like Champlain, Le Clerq and others, seem to have been unacquainted with Hakluyt's account. Most of the works on Canada are more or less confused so far as regards the expedition of Roberval. This shows again how important statements in writers of his class may long lie unnoticed and, practically, unknown.

"Father Charlevoix, whose veracity is usually held in moderate esteem, in his *History of New France*, says, in a passage, the exactness of which in other respects may be acknowledged, that Roberval 'sent one of his pilots named Alphonse, born in Portugal, according to some, and in Gallica according to others, to seek above Newfoundland a way to the East Indies.'

"This nationality, beyond the Pyrenees, might have been based thoughtlessly on the name Xanctoigne, printed in Hakluyt, and which might have been taken for that of the Spanish city of Santona, a little port on the coast of Asturies, instead of recognizing in the same, as is proper, not, indeed, the French province of Saintonge as is commonly supposed, but a village or district (*pagus*) of the same name near Cognac.

"A sure and precise indication of the French origin of our pilot is afforded in a little work presenting a general *portulani* of the then known world, published for the first time by Jean de Marnef, to whom Mellin de Saint-Gelais had remitted a copy thereof, difficult to be had since the death of the skillful mariner, as a preliminary advertisement of the publisher makes it known printed on the back of the frontispiece. The work has for a title *Les Voyages Avantureux du Capitaine Jan Alfonce Sainctongeois.* It is a little volume in quarto numbering sixty-eight leaves, without date, having appended thereto several pages of ciphers of tables of the declension of the sun, put in by order of Oliver Bisselin, 'and the printing thereof finished by the end of the month of April, in the year 1550.' On the *verso* of the sixty-eighth and last leaf, is to be read this epilogue: 'End of the present book, composed and ordered by Jan Alphonce, an experienced pilot in the things narrated in this book, a native of the country of Xainctonge, near the city of Cognac. Done at the request of

Vincent Aymard, merchant of the country of Piedmont, Maugis Vumenot, merchant of Honfleur, writing for him.'

"This last mention reveals, to all appearances, the real author of this abridged and unfaithful edition, which through error, Brunet ascribes to Saint-Gelais himself. This is not the only inadvertency of the learned bibliographer. He seemed to find in the preliminary advertisement of *Jan de Marnef to the Reader*, the certain indication that Mellin de Saint-Gelais was still living at the unexpressed date of the earliest edition, and he concludes thereupon that this edition is anterior to October, 1558, the time of the death of the Saintongeois poet. It was sufficient, however, to read the following page, which faces a sonnet signed *Sc. de S. M.* (evidently *Scévole de Saint-Marthe*), addressed particularly To the Shade of Saingelais, to be assured, on the contrary, of the exactness of the date of 1559, which is to be found at the end of the annexed tables devoted to Bisselin. It is true that certain copies showed on the back of the frontispiece, instead of the advertisement of Marnef, the royal privilege, dated March 7, 1557, but it is immediately followed by the mention, 'printing finished May, 2, 1559.' There can remain no doubt on this point.

"Besides the original edition in quarto, which we have just pointed out, there exists another of the same size, brought out at Rouen in 1578, by Thomas Mallard, having also the tables of Bisselin, but without the pieces of verse in honor of Allefonsce, which are to be seen at the head of the first edition. Still another edition of Paris, 1598, octavo, is mentioned.

"*M. Leon Genrin* who in his *Navigateurs Français* has given a notice of Allephonsce de Saintongeois, has inserted in the same a general analysis of the volume.

"*Les Voyages Avantureux de Jan Alfonce*, written by Maugis Vumenot, no more than the *Excellent ruttier*, translated by Richard Hakluyt, can be considered as good specimens of the original work of this pilot, preserved in manuscript in the Imperial Library at Paris, and which has already been pointed out by *Antoine de Leon Pinello* in his Oriental and Occidental Library, a sort of bibliographical work, to be used with caution, but full of useful information. This manuscript forms a volume in folio, entitled *Cosmographie*, and is dedicated to King Francis I. It presents a text quite extensive, in which it intercalates the successive draughts of the coasts that are described therein. M. Pierre Margry, who intends to comprise it in the collection of documents which he is preparing, to be called *Les Origines Historiques de la France d'outre-mer*, and who has shown us a copy of the same entirely in his own hand, has ground for declaring that the edition of *Maugis Vumenot* is only a worthless abridgement; and the fragment translated by Hakluyt, is disfigured throughout by the most singular mistakes.

"The original volume ends with the following epilogue : 'End of the Cosmography made and composed by us, *Jehan Allefonsce* and *Paulin Sécalart,* captains and pilots of vessels residing in the city of Rochelle, in the *Saint Jehan des Pretz* street, opposite the church of the said *Saint Jehan,* the 24th day of the month of November, the year 1545, finished by me, *Paulin Sécalart,* cosmographer of Honfleur, desiring to do service to your Royal Majesty, which will be the end of the present book 1545.'

"One may conjecture from these indications that *Jehan Allefonsce,* who wrote his *Cosmography* in 1544, after forty-eight years of navigation, with the assistance of a secretary, a pilot like himself, *Paulin Sécalart, poor and loyal,* was overtaken by death before having put the last touch to his work, and that this very *Paulin Sécalart* of Honfleur, finished it alone, the twenty-fourth of November in the very house where they stayed together in Rochelle.

"In his long maritime career, Captain *Jean Allefonsce* sailed in Portuguese vessels, having in particular commanded a vessel belonging to *Edouard de Paz*. He had naturally received from the ship owners, as a nickname, the national designation of *Francez*, which *M. de Varnhagen* has taken for his Portuguese family name, in speaking of the royal letters of safe-conduct in favor of the said ' *Joannis Affonsi Francez qui erat expertus in viagiis ad Brasiliarias insulas*,' whom they tried to recall, and to whom was promised that he should not be sought again or prosecuted by virtue of the laws framed against those mariners who abandoned Portugal to take service in foreign countries, or who abandoned, without leave, the Portuguese possessions in America.

"When calling to mind with what savage rigor the Portuguese government of that time dealt with the foreigners who dared to violate what it called its exclusive rights by conquest, one easily conceives that letters of safe-conduct were indispensable for foreigners as well as natives who consented to return to Portugal. Offers of this nature do not by any means imply a denial of the Spanish nationality of Solis, nor the French nationality of Allefonsce."

APPENDIX.

APPENDIX.

I.

Page 5.— In the chapter on the Northmen the author has taken Dr. Kohl on his own ground, and considered the force of each particular expression with reference to the points at issue. And in this use of the language of the Sagas their historic character is conceded. Still, the right to make such a use of the language of the narratives has been questioned by a writer in the *North American Review* for July, 1869.

It will be remembered that Mr. Bancroft, in his History, took the position that the Sagas relating to America were *mythological* in form, and thus affected to dispose of them very cheaply. He has probably regretted it many times since, as the position in question is so unfavorable to a reputation for candor.

And now the writer referred to comes in a recent number of the *Review* above-mentioned, and, in the course of a long article upon the author's work entitled *The Pre-Columbian Discovery of America by the Northmen*, sets forward a new theory which gives the Sagas a poetical origin.

While scouting Mr. Bancroft's mythological view, the critic adopts one of his own which is but little better, and which seeks to take away the plain historical character of the writings in question. His rather novel view is, that the Sagas originally existed in the form of popular ballads, which were afterwards reduced to prose, and consequently are not to be used as they have been by Dr. Kohl and the author; and as in fact the best authorities are accustomed to use them.

His manner of proceeding is as follows: Turning to the *Heimskringla*, or *The Sea-Kings of Norway*, by Snorre Sturleson, he thinks that he finds evidence there that that work was largely composed from ballads and old songs. Having settled this, he repairs to the Sagas relating to America, and claims to find the same characteristics in their construction.

He errs, however, at the outset; for his declaration that the Heimskringla was largely composed of songs is flatly denied by the most competent authority; while, if his assumption *were* true, he would not be justified in applying the same rule to the American Sagas, which, internally, show no signs of a lyrical origin, any more than the *Landnama*, which is the equivalent of the Dooms-day Book, and yet contains poetical fragments. A ballad incorporated in an Icelandic Saga affords no more evidence of its poetic origin than some scrap of song quoted in an American history.

It is very gratifying to observe what general acceptance the Sagas have already gained, as well as to notice the ease with which such objections have always been brushed away, especially when supported by the hand-book learning of the critic in the *North American Review*.

II.

Page 66.—Having expressed the belief that Thevet gave the wrong Indian name of the river Norumbega, I here state the authority. The original may be seen on page 493 of Lescarbot's *Nouvelle France*, ed. 1612. The following is from Erondelle's translation (ed. 1609, page 46):

"Therefore without alleaging that, which the first writers (Spaniards and Portingals) haue said, I will recite that which is in the last booke, intitled *The Universal Historie of the West Indies*, Printed at *Douay* the last yeere 1607, in the place where he speaketh of *Norombega:* For in reporting this, I shall haue also said that which the first haue written, from whom they haue had it.

"Moreouer, towards the North (saith the Author, after he had spoken of Virginia) "is *Norombega*, which is known well enough by reason of a faire towne, and a great riuer, though it is not found from whence it hath his name: for the

Barbarians doe call it *Agguncia:* at the mouth of this river is an Island very fit for fishing. The region that goeth along the sea doth abound in fish, and toward New France there is a great number of wilde beasts, and is verie commodious for hunting; the inhabitance doe liue in the same maner as they of New France." If this beautifull Towne hath ever beene in nature, I faine would know who hath pulled it doune: For there is but cabanes here and there made with pearkes, and couered with barkes of trees, or with skinnes, and both the river and the place inhabited is called *Pemptegoet,* and not *Agguncia.* The riuer (sauing the tide) is scarce as the riuer of *Oyse.* And there can be no great riuer on that coast, because there are not lands sufficient to produce them, by reason of the great riuer of *Canada* which runneth like this coast, and is not fourescore leagues distant from that place in crossing the lands, which from elsewhere received manie riuers falling from those parts which are toward *Norombega:* At the entrie whereof, it is so far from hauing but one Island, that rather the number thereof is almost infinite, for as much as this riuer enlarging it selfe like the Greek *Lambda* Λ, the mouth whereof is all full of isles, whereof there is one of them lying very farre off (and the foremost) in the sea [Mt. Desert?] which is high and remarkable aboue the others."

This name, Agguncia, therefore came from the Spaniards and Portuguese, from whom the author quoted by Lescarbot took it. This author was Wytfliet, whose edition of *Ptolemaicæ Augmentum* of 1607, contains an account of the West Indies. On page 68 I have allowed that Wytfliet copied a few lines from Thevet, but that concession was based upon the edition of his work published in 1603. The edition of 1607, however, is more full, and shows distinctly that Wytfliet, as Lescarbot indicates, quoted from early Spanish and Portuguese writers. From this source Thevet was supplied with his own false information. Than this nothing need be more clear. Thevet was also probably acquainted with the abstracts of Allfonsce's work at the time he published his *Cosmographie*. The monk was also the personal friend of Cartier, Roberval, and Rabelais; the latter being, in turn, the friend of the eulogist of Allfonsce, if not of Allfonsce himself. With such friends at command, Thevet could easily have written on the subject of Norumbega: yet he had no excuse for writing so poorly.

III.

Page 78.— In the paper on Thevet I have dealt with him only as he appears in his *Cosmographie;* yet it must be remembered that his *Antarctic*

France covers the same alleged voyage along the American coast to Labrador. This work was published in 1558, but it differs from the first mentioned, inasmuch as it has nothing to say about Norumbega, of which region Thevet at that time knew nothing. And still, according to his *Cosmographie*, published in 1575, he made a voyage to the coast of Norumbega in 1556. It is therefore plain that his account was derived from the relations of others, to which he found access at a later time. These accounts were by those writers to whom Lescarbot alludes.

Whoever takes up his *Antarctic France* will perceive that Thevet appears to be describing an imaginary tour to a great extent, and that he employs his peculiar method in order to excite interest.

After leaving Brazil, he takes the reader to the coast of Mexico, and then in imagination, sends him through the straits of Darien to Peru, not knowing that a ship would there encounter the firm land. After describing Peru, he returns to Florida, and, in order to prolong his voyage to Labrador, invents an "unfavorable wind." This takes him to every part of the north, except Norumbega, of which he then knew nothing.

In a word, it is as absurd to suppose from Thevet's accounts that he visited Maine, as to argue that he visited Africa, Quebec and Peru.

IV.

Page 81.— It is very curious that in Charlevoix we find an account of Unipeds. After stating the story related by a St. Malo captain to the effect that the well known Indian Donnacona told him that he once went on a voyage to a country where he saw men with but "one leg and thigh," he says:

"It is, moreover, very strange that the story of one-legged men should be renewed quite recently by a young Esquimaux girl, captured in 1717, and brought to Mr. De Courtemanche, on the coast of Labrador, where she still was in 1720, when I reached Quebec   *   *   Also she said that among her countrymen there was another kind of men, who had only one leg, one thigh, and a very large foot, two hands on the same arm, a broad body, a flat head, small eyes, scarcely any nose, and a small mouth; and that they were always in a bad humor." *Shea's Charlevoix*, vol. I, p. 124–25.

V.

Page 99.—Misrepresentations of Allfonsce have already been pointed out, but it is proper here to cite Lescarbot, and explain the origin of his views, which have done the French captain some harm, in the estimation of those not conversant with the facts of the case. In Erondelle (page 47) we read as follows:

" True it is that a sea Captaine, named *Iohn Alfonse*, of *Xaintonge*, in the relation of his adventurous voiages, hath written, that hauing passed Saint *Iohn's* Iland (which I take for the same that I haue called heeretofore the Isle of *Bacaillos*) "the coast turneth to the West, and West Southwest, as far as the riuer of *Norumbergu*, newly discovered (saith he) by the Portugais and Spaniards, which is in 30 degrees : adding that this riuer hath, at the entrie thereof many Iles, bankes and rockes, and that fifteen or twenty leagues within it is built a great towne where the people be small and blackish like them of the Indies, and are clothed with skinnes whereof they haue abundance of all sorts. Item that the bank of New Foundland endeth there : and that the riuer being passed, the coast turneth to the West and West Northwest, aboue 250 leagues towards a countrie where there is both townes and castels." But I see very little or no truth at all in all the discourses of this man; and well may he call his voiges adventurous, not for him, who was never in the hundreth part of the places he describeth (at least it is easy so to thinke) but for those that will follow the wais which he willeth mariners to follow. For if the said riuer of Norombega be in thirty degrees, it must needs be in *Florida*, which is contrarie to all of them that have ever written of it, and to the verie truth itselfe." (*Lescarbot's Nouvelle France*, p. 495). Now this might at first seem conclusive, yet we must remember that it is not Allfonsce that he quotes from but the travesty upon his *Hydrography*, worked up with spicy additions, and alterations after his death. The removal of Norumbega to the latitude of 30° N., is only equaled by Hakluyt's blunder by which he makes the pilot speak of the region of St. Lawrence as a country producing *figs*.

But if Allfonsce had actually written in this way in regard to Norumbega and the region in general, he certainly would have been entitled to no credit; yet it must be remembered that Lescarbot really knew nothing of this navigator, who is not at all responsible for the "Adventurous Voyages" passed off under his name. The extract given from his *Hydrography*, on page 93, shows that he limits the southern border of Norumbega to about latitude 42° N., and therefore the statement of the Adventurous Voyages, which puts the river in latitude 30° N., is not his.

This statement of the compiler is equaled only by the blunder of Hakluyt (see *ante*, p. 99), who transports the fig tree from Yucatan to the banks of the St. Lawrence.

And it is a very noticeable fact that the Quebec Literary and Historical Society has perpetuated the blunders of Hakluyt, by turning his translation back into French. Hence on page 86 of *Voyages du Découverter au Canada*, we find that country spoken of as follows: *et cette terre peut produire des Figues et des Poires.*

While these things stand on record it will be idle for any one to attempt to impeach Jean Allfonsce, especially in his latitudes, as his perfect knowledge of the astrolabe rendered his calculations every way worthy of trust.

VI.

Page 102.— The voyage of Maldonado is here referred to in the note, and it is interesting to observe in that connection that the ideas of the Spaniards were often very confused on the subject of Baccalaos. In the French edition of Gomera (1569, page 49), we read:

"There is a large tract of land that projects itself pointwise into the sea, which tract is called Baccaleos. Its greatest altitude is forty-four and a half degrees."

VII.

Page 111.— The author expected ere this, to have received a copy of Allfonsce's work, made from the original manuscript, which probably shows the extent of his observations on the New England coast. That he visited Maine appears not unlikely, for the reason that some knowledge of the physical characteristics of Penobscot bay is *attributed* to him in the extract by Lescarbot.

We also find a good reason why he should have visited the entire New England coast, in the fact that Roberval was entitled to this whole region by the terms of his patent. One of the titles conferred upon him by the king of France was "Lord of Norumbega." Mr. Parkman, in his *Pioneers of New France* (p. 197), disputes this, and cites a copy of Roberval's commission, made from the original, which does not allude to it, and suggests that the titles were invented by Charlevoix " for the sake of their bearing on the boundary disputes with England in his own day." But he is very properly reminded by Mr. Shea, in his *Charlevoix* (p. 129), that he has confounded the *commission* with *patent.* The latter is given in full by Lescarbot (p. 397, ed. 1618).

Roberval was, according to the royal authority, "Lord of Norumbega," and thus the priority of *all* English patents of the New England coast is technically quashed. Allfonsce in visiting the coast probably had reference to his employer's interests. Yet, while we are certain that he visited Massachusetts bay, we cannot just now positively affirm anything more.

VIII.

Page 113.— The proof of Cartier's fourth voyage is not so clear as might be wished. Nor does it show that Cartier performed any other office than that of a messenger. So far as the account goes, Roberval may have had a ship with him, in which he returned without receiving any aid from Cartier. We learn of this matter from the accounts of the difficulties that occurred in the way of settlement between the two leaders after their return, when Francis the First appointed Robert Legoupil arbiter of the case. Ferland says in his *Cours d'Histoire* (p. 45) that

"According to Lescarbot, Francis I, unable to send the aid solicited, and desiring to employ Roberval in the army, conveyed his will to him through Jacques Cartier, who was ordered to undertake a fourth voyage to Canada, to bring back to France the wretched remnants of the colony. Official documents inform us that this voyage lasted eight months."

The documents upon which he bases his opinion are those contained in the publication of the Quebec Literary and Historical Society for 1862. Alluding to Cartier, they speak of "Eight months that he has been to return and bring the said Roberval in the said Canada." And again, of " having set out in the fall of 1543 on his fourth voyage Cartier would have wintered in Canada, and would have left it at the end of April or in the beginning of May, 1544." Thevet reports that Roberval was murdered in Paris.

IX.

Page 113.— According to the Quebec Literary and Historical Society's publications, 1862 (p. 113), M. Manet, author of *Biographie des Malouins Célèbres*, holds:

"That Roberval after restoring his fort sent Jean Alphonse de Xaintonge north of New Foundland to seek a passage to the Indies [see *ante* p. 104.] The latter ran up as far as 52° N., and went no farther. We are not told how long he was engaged on this voyage, but we may conjecture that he found de Roberval no longer in Canada, inasmuch as he makes a report to Jacques Cartier."

On this the Quebec editor remarks:

"If the Pilot John Alphonse made a report of his discoveries to Cartier, it must have been on a fourth voyage made by the latter in the summer of 1543, or after his return to Brittany."

But in regard to this report by Allfonsce to Cartier we at present know nothing; while on page, 105 we have already shown that the voyage to the north must, with good reason, have been made in the summer of 1542, as *after* that time Roberval could have had no ship to spare. M. Manet's remark, that, on his return, Allfonsce found Roberval gone, therefore, has no foundation, and indicates that M. Manet really knew nothing about the matter. At least he gives no authority for his opinion, which leaves us to infer that he had none to give.

X.

In connection with this subject, a point brought forward in the volume devoted to the Popham Celebration may be properly noticed. Mr. Sewall says:

"Monhegan, signifying an island of the main, earliest appears in the panorama of the historic scene of English life and enterprise on New England shores. Pedro Menedez, Governor of Florida, in dispatches forwarded by him to the Court of Spain, [1588] tells Philip II, 'that in July of the year, the English were inhabiting an island in latitude 43°, eight leagues from the land, where the Indians were very numerous.' It was the story of 'Carlos Morea, a Spaniard, who had learned the facts in London and communicated them to Menedez.' There can hardly be a doubt that Monhegan Island was the spot occupied by these English dwellers in the New

World. Indeed it was only in August, three years before, that near this spot, the largest ship of Sir Humphrey Gilbert struck."

The author of the above was led into error by mistaking the language of Bancroft, who puts the place of the shipwreck *not* south of " the latitude of Wiscasset," without giving the longitude. Gilbert's first ship was lost on the Isle of Sable, east of Nova Scotia. (See Hakluyt, vol. III, p. 164, ed. 1600.)

As regards the other point, we see, by referring to the full relation, that it was simply a sailor's report, and undoubtedly grew out of the accounts of Sir Humphrey Gilbert's voyage and the attempts that preceded it. Besides, we have no further report on the subject, though Menedez says that he had already sent a ship to reconnoitre the coast as far as San Juan, in latitude 39° N., and promises to write again should anything become known. He speaks as follows:

" There is a sailor, Carlos Morea, who says it is certain that, in the island of San Juan, near the Bacallaos, the English have a settlement; for two years ago, being in London, a vessel arrived there, on which came a friend of his, who told him positively that they were inhabiting an island, in forty-three degrees of latitude, eight leagues from the main land ; that there were great numbers of Indians there, of which he also feels certain.

I will inform your majesty how it is in the manner stated."

It may also be added that the sailor himself appears uncertain of his latitude, by seeming to make the island in question that of *San Juan*. (See *Sailing Directions of Henry Hudson*, p. 47). Note also that the Spanish used "Baccaleos" loosely; that Monhegan is ten *miles*, instead of eight *leagues* from the land. The sailor probably meant Nantucket. Mr. Buckingham Smith originally translated the statement, but framed no theory on the subject.

INDEX.

Acadie, 72, 73.
Affonsi, Joannis, 121, see Allfonsce.
Agassiz, 85 n.
Agguncia, 66, 128.
Agoncy, 64, 66.
Allefonsce, see Allfonsce.
Allfonsce, sonnet to, Frontispiece; pilot of Roberval, 92; went to Canada, 92, 113; his Hydrography, 92, 93, 108; views of north-west passage, 94; sailed under the Portuguese, 95; discovered Massachusetts bay, 96, 105; voyage to the north, 105; time at sea, 107; place of birth, 108; in prison, 108; time of death, 108; his eulogist, 109; high character, 110; in advance of his times, 111; biography of, 112; claimed by the Portuguese, 113; his Ruttier, 114, 119; French origin, 115; Avantureux voyages, 116, 119; date of Hydrography, 118; Cosmography, 119, 120; place of death, 120; sailed in Portuguese vessels, 121; left Portuguese service, 121; 97, 98, 99, 100, 101, 102, 103, 129, 131, 132, 134, 137.

Alphonse, Iohn, 97, 107, see Allfonsce.
American Antiquarian Society, 85 n.
Angouleme, 72, 73.
Angouleme, the bishop of, 109 n.
Annals of Florida, 61.
Antarctic France, Singularities of, 74, 130.
Antiquitates Americanæ, quoted, 11, 15, 16, 26, 27.
Appendix, 123.
Arembec, 49, 50, 51, see Norumbega.
Arias, Gomez, 102 n.
Arnœ-Magnean Collection, 18.
Arnodie, 69, 70, 71.
Asia, 41, 97.
Asturies, 115.
Atlantic, the south, 76.
Aymard, Vincent, 117.

Baccalaos, 52, 60, 71, 102 n, 134, 139, 140.
Bancroft, Mr., 125, 139.
Barcia, 61.
Bardsen, chronicle of, 32, 34, 37, 38.
Barry, his history, 91.
Bay of Fundy, 14, 73.
Bear Island, 15, 17, 19.
Bear killed, 15.
Bearse, Mr. J. Y., 87 n, 88 n.

142 INDEX.

Belle Isle, 97.
Beriah's ledge, 87 n.
Biddle, 53 n, 58 n, 98 n.
Biographic Universelle, 74.
Bishop Eric, 26, 27.
Bisselin, Oliver, 116, 118.
Blue Hills, 83.
Blunt's Coast Pilot, 24.
Boston, 9, 21, 24.
Boston Harbor, 24, 25.
Brattahlid, 37 n.
Brazil, 108, 130.
Brereton, 91.
Bretons, 72.
Brevoort, J. Carson, 94 n.
Brunet, 117.
Buzzard's Bay, 20, 24.
Bygd, East, of Greenland, 33, 35.

Cabot, 54, 58 n, 101.
Cabots, the, 91.
Camden Hills, 67.
Canada, 64, 69, 97, 128.
Cape Ann, 96.
Cape Arenas, 71 n, 90.
Cape Breton, 42, 45, 47, 49, 51, 55, 71.
Cape Cod, 6, 7, 9, 10, 13, 15, 17, 19, 20, 42, 71 n, 82, 84, 85, 85 n, 87, 89 n, 90, 96.
Cape de Bas, 50, 56, 57.
Cape De Bas Harbor, 50.
Cape de Mucha isles, 67.
Cape de Sper, 51.
Cape Farewell, 38.
Cape of the Isles, 67.
Cape Sable, 14.
Cape St. Mary, 90.
Carpont, 97.
Cartier, Jacques, 100, 113, 129, 136.
Cathay, 95.
Charlevoix, Pere, 103, 115, 135.
Chatham, 87 n.
Chicora, 53.
China, 52.

Clay Pounds, 89 n.
Cognac, 105, 115, 116.
Cosa, map of, 41, 42.
Cosmographie Universelle, 45, 64.
Courtmauche, 131.
Crabb's ledge, 87 n.
Crignon, Pierre, 44, 45.
Crosses, Thorvald's, 9, 10.
Crossness, 9.
Cortereal, 91.
Cortez, 62.

Danes, 35 n.
Danish government, expedition of, 33.
Darien, 130.
Davezac, M., 93, 100, 112.
De Prato, 56.
Dieppe, 44.
Discovery, north-western, 57.
Doane, Mr. John, 85 n, 86.
Dominus Vobiscum, 49.
Donnacona, 131.
Drake, his history of Boston, 92.
Drogeo, 40, 41.

East Indies, 104, 115.
Eastham, 86 n.
Edouard du Paz, 121.
Einersfiord, 36.
El Pico, 61 n.
Eleste, 38.
England, 57, 58.
England, King of, 62, n.
English ship, 53, 62.
Englishmen, first in Maine, 52.
Eric, Saga of, 18.
Ericsfiord, 37.
Ericson, Thorvald, 82.
Erondelle, 132.
Europeans, first on coast of Maine, 25.
Explorations in Greenland, 33.
Explorers of America, 40.

INDEX. 143

Ferland, 136.
Fig Tree, 99 n.
Finnboge, 27, 28.
Fiöll, 23.
Fishing vessels, 50, 55.
Fjeld, 23.
Florida, 45, 49, 63, 64, 75, 77, 94, 98, 99, 132.
Fluvium Lande, 36.
Folsom, his History, 90.
Fox Island, 66.
France, 105.
Francis I, 136.
French Pilots, 72.
Freydis, 26, 27, 28.

Garda, 37 n.
Gastaldi, 45, 65.
Genrin, M. Leon, 118.
Geographie, Bulletin of, 112.
Georges, shoals of, 42, 88 n, 89 n, 90.
Gilbert, Sir Humphrey, 45, 78, 91, 101, 139.
Goodwin Sands, 89, n.
Gosnold, 85 n, 86, 88 n, 90, 91, 96.
Graah, Captain, Expedition of, 33.
Grand Bay, 97.
Grand River, 64.
Green Mountains, 67.
Greenland, 8; names of, 30, 31, 32; settled, 32; lost, 32, 34, 35 n, 38, 39, 77, 84.
Gronlandia Antiqua, 84.
Gudrida, 7.
Gulf of Maine, 7, 21, 22.
Gulf Stream, 56.
Gurnet Point, 9, 10.

Hakluyt, 41, 42, 46, 47, 48, 51, 57, 58, 97, 98, 99, 100, 103, 107, 113, 115, 119, 120, 132, 139.
Havre, 75.
Heimskringla, 126.

Helge, 27, 28.
Helluland, 15, 18.
Henlestate, 38.
Henry VIII, 41.
Heriulfsness, 36, 37, n.
Herrera, 52, 54, 58, 59.
Hien, 36.
Highland Light, 89, n.
Honfleur, 120.
Hop, 22, 23, 24.
Huarfs, 38.
Hudson, Henry, 140; Sailing Directions of, 38 n.
Hudson river, 67.

Iceland, 21.
Imperial Library of Paris, 92.
Indians, 61.
Island, 15, 17, 19.
Isle Nauset, 85 n.
Isle of Demons, 76, 83.
Isle of St. Croix, 71.
Isle Thevet, 71.
Islesboro, 67.
Italy, 59.

James Head, 87 n.
Jöcher, his Lexicon, 74, 75.
Juan Florentin, 61.
Judi, 69.

Karlsefne, Thorfinn, 6, 7, 8, 9, 10, 15, 18, 20, 22, 26, 42, 83.
Kennebec, 14.
Kialarness, 6, 7, 10, 11, 15, 20, 21.
King Henry VIII, 50, 58.
Kohl, Dr. J. H., 5, 6, 7, 9, 10, 11, 12, 15, 17, 18, 20, 21, 22, 23, 25, 26, 28, 30, 31, 40, 42, 45, 48, 52, 53, 56, 63, 74, 78, 79, 81, 84, 92, 101, 125.

Labadists, 86, 130.
Labrador, 15, 104, 105.
Lancaster Sound, 39.
Landnama, 126.
Lardner, Dr., 98 n.

La Roquette, 76.
Lebrija, 113.
Le Clerc, 103.
Legoupil, Robert, 136.
Leif, 8.
Lelewell, 31 ; his *Moyan Age*, 36, 37, 38, 40.
Lery, his Brazil, 75.
Lescarbot, 127, 129, 135, 136.
Lodmundfiord, 37, *n*.
Long Island, 66, 67.
Long Island Historical Society of, 87, 94, *n*.
Lord of Norumbega, 135.

MacDonald, 134.
Madoc, 91.
Maine, 10, 11, 12, 13, 14, 15, 17, 20, 102 *n*; expedition to, 21 ; country of, 22, 25, 40, 41, 83, 111.
Maine Historical Society, 5.
Maldonado, 101.
Malebarre, 89.
Mallard, Thomas, 118.
Manamoit point, 87 *n*, 88 *n*.
Manet, M., 137.
Maps, of Cape Cod, 89 ; Spanish and Portuguese, 90 ; Icelandic, 41 ; Cosa's, 41.
Margry, M. Pierre, 93, 94, 95, 99 *n*, 100, 103, 110, 112, 119.
Markland, 6, 7, 12, 15, 16, 17, 25 *n*.
Marnef, Jean de, 116, 118.
Marot, 109.
Martha's Vineyard, 88 *n*.
Martyr, Peter, 44.
Mary of Guilford, 42, 47, 48, 52, 53, 55, 56, 58, 59, 62.
Massachusetts Bay, 100, 104 ; discovery of, 80 ; by the Northmen; by Karlsefne, 83 ; shown by map of Stephanius, 84, 92 ; by Allfonsce, 92, 95; date of his discovery, 107.

Massacre by Freydis, 28.
Menedez, Pedro, 138.
Mercator, 34, 67.
Meta Incognita, 48.
Mexico, 72, 77, 130.
Milton Blue Hills, 23, 25.
Monhegan, Isle of, 138.
Montana Verde, 67.
Monument to Verrazano, 60.
Morea, Carlos, 138, 139.
Morse, his Gazetteer, 87 *n*.
Mount Desert, 68, 70, 128.
Mount Hope Bay, 23.
Munder, 37 *n*.

Nantucket, 42, 87, 88, 140.
Nauset Beach, 80 *n*.
Nauset Harbor, 57 *n*.
Nestorian bishop, 76.
New Brunswick, 51, 65, 73.
New Castile, 61 *n*.
New England, 27, 40, 45, 46, 72, 81 ; coast, 100.
New Foundland, 42, 46, 47, 48, 49, 50, 51, 60, 63, 103, 115, 132.
New France, 44, 98, 99.
New Hampshire, 17.
New Hampshire, 65.
New-land, 104.
Newport, 101 *n*.
Newport Mill, 27.
New York, 101 *n*.
New York, bay of, 106.
North American Review, 125.
North Carolina, 53.
Normans, 55.
Northern Antiquarians, 33.
Northmen, the, 22, 82, 84, 101, 126.
North-west passage, 50.
Norumbega, 42, 44, 45, 46, 47, 48, 49, 60, 65, 76, 98, 127, 130, 132, 135.
Nova Scotia, 6, 7, 12, 13, 14, 16, 17, 18, 19, 45, 46, 57, 96.

INDEX. 145

Ortelius, 34.
Oviedo, 53, 54.
Oyse, the river, 128.

Palfrey, his History, 81, 91.
Parkman, 135.
Pemptegoet, 128.
Penobscot river, 45, 64, 66, 70.
Pentagruel, the Prince, 107, 111.
Peru, 130.
Piedmont, pilot of, 53, 58, 60, 117.
Pinello, Antoine de Leon, 119.
Pirate, 62 n.
Piscataqua, 79.
Plymouth, 9, 20, 21, 82.
Point Care, 85 n, 87 n.
Point Gilbert, 86, 87 n, 89 n.
Poitiers, 108, 111.
Porto Rico, 52, 54, 55, 57, 58.
Portugal, 122.
Provincetown, 21.
Purchas, 49, 51.
Pyrenees, the, 115.

Quebec, 103, 132; Literary Society of, 134, 136.

Rabelais, 109, 129.
Race Point, 21.
Rafn, 12, 24, 27.
Ramusio, 44, 58, 61.
Rhode Island, 7, 20, 21.
Ribero, 63.
Rio Janerio, 74.
Roberval, 97, 103, 104, 105, 106, 113, 114, 115, 129, 135, 163.
Rochelle, 103, 113.
Ronsard, the poet, 119 n.
Rouen, 118.
Ruscelli, 90.
Rut, John, 42, 47, 51, 52, 54, 56, 57, 59, 60, 65, 98 n, 101.
Rye Beach, 65.

Saga, 21, 25, 42, 82, 126.
Saguenay, 95, 103.

Saine Terre, M., 107.
Saingelais, the Shade of, 117.
St. Croix, 73, 79.
St. Domingo, 57.
Saint-Gelais, Mellin de, 106, 109 n, 117.
St. German, 57.
Saint Jehan des Pretz street, 120.
St. John's, 50, 55, 56, 57, 60, 103, 105.
St. Juan, 53.
St. Lawrence, 46, 100, 106.
St. Malo, 131.
Saint Marthe, Scevole de, 117.
St. Thomas, 40 n.
Saintonge, province of, 115.
Saintongeois, poet, 117.
Sampson, the, 42, 48, 51, 56, 57.
San Antonio, 67.
San Juan, 139.
Santona, 115.
Schoodic Point, 67.
Sea-Kings of Norway, 126.
Secalart, Paulin, 120, 121.
Sewall, Mr., 138.
Shea, 131, 135.
Situate Harbor, 24.
Skolnus, 91.
Slut's Bush, 86, 87.
Smith, Buckingham, 61 n, 140.
Solis, Jean Diaz de, 113, 122.
South America, 72, 74.
Southey, his Brazil, 74, n.
Spain, 62.
Spaniards, 53.
Stephanius, Sigurdus, his map, 84, 89 n.
Stevens, Mr., 41, 61.
Straumfiord, 20, 24.
Sturleson, Snorre, 126.
Surveys, geological, 42.

Tartary, 94, 97.
Thevet, André, 63, 64, 65, 66, 67, 68, 72, 78, 101, 127, 129.

19

Torfæus, work on Old Greenland, 32, 33, 34.
Thorfinn, account of, 18 ; narrative of, 18, 24.
Thorhall, 20, 21, 83.
Thorlacius, Theodore, 34, 39.
Thorne, 41, 58.
Thorvald, 8, 9, 28.
Two Chateaux, 76.

Unipeds, 83, 131.
United States, 47.
Utopia, 110.

Varnhagen, M. de, 121.
Vega, Garcilaso de la, 102 n.
Venice, 111.
Verra, 11, 106.
Verrazano, 58, 59, 61, 89 n, 101.
Villegagnon, 75 n.
Vinland, 7, 8, 20, 25 n, 26, 27, 28, 89.

Visscher's map, 90.
Voyage of John Rut, 42.
Vumenot, Maugis, 117, 119, 120.

Webb's Island, 87 n.
Weirs, 76.
West Indies, 44, 55, 56, 62.
Williamson's History of Maine, 66.
Wonderstrand, 20.
Woomskiold, 33.
Wytfliet's Ptolemaicæ Augmentum, 68, 129.

Yucatan, 99 n, 132.

Zeni, the, 32 ; map of, 32, 34 n, 35, 36, 37, 38, 42, 91.
Zeno, Antonio, 30, 39.
Zeno Brothers, 30.
Zeno, Nicolo, 30.
Zurla, 38.

ERRATA.

Page 12, line seven, for *indtif*, read *indtil ;* for *utque*, read *usque*.
Page 32, line ten, for *to rightly apply*, read, *to apply rightly*.
Page 62, note, for *clothes*, read *cloths*.
Page 80, line twelve, for *has*, read *have*.
Page 88, note, for *Mass*., read *N. E.*

www.ingramcontent.com/pod-product-compliance
Lightning Source LLC
Chambersburg PA
CBHW022129160426
43197CB00009B/1207